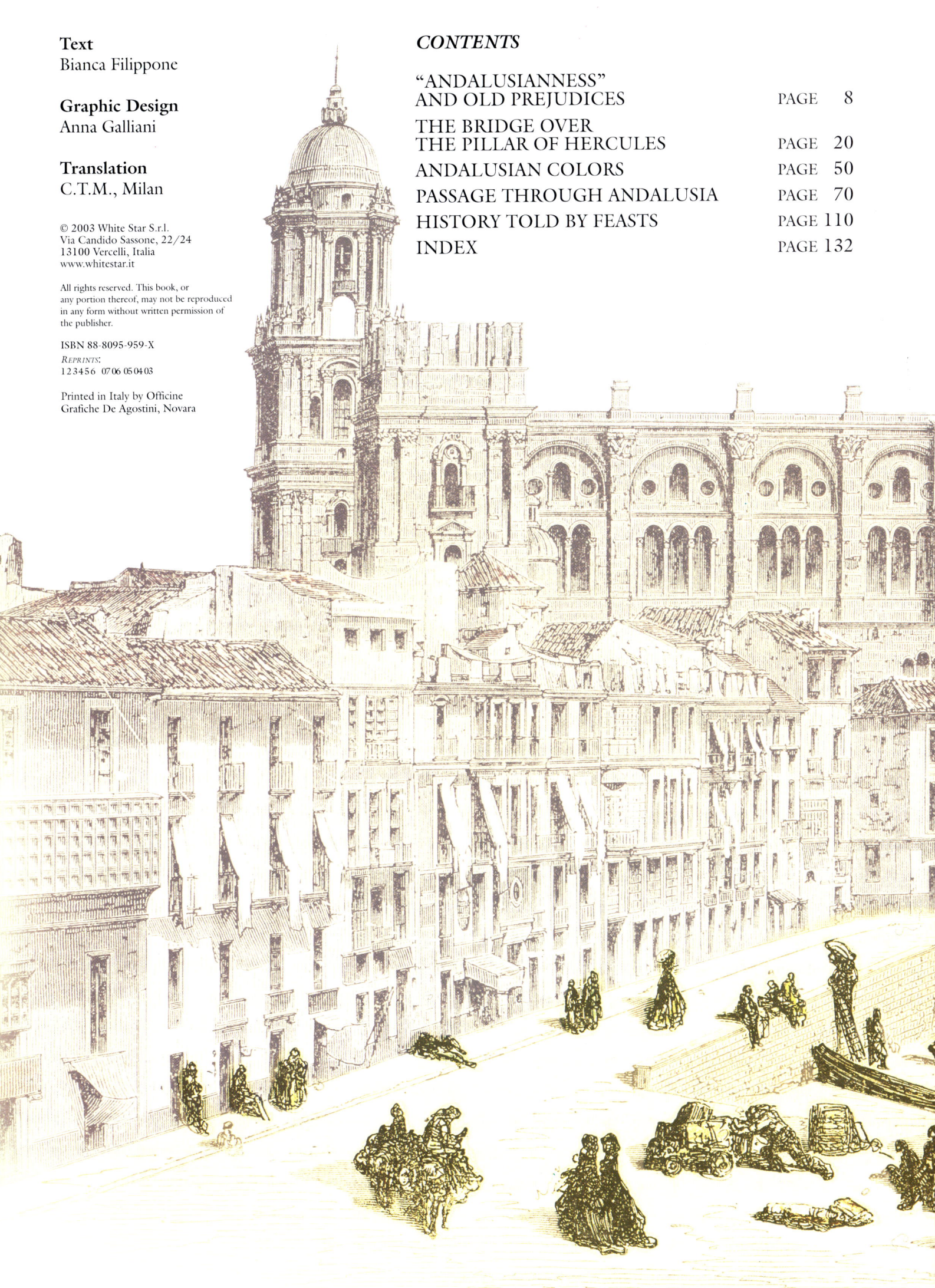

Text
Bianca Filippone

Graphic Design
Anna Galliani

Translation
C.T.M., Milan

© 2003 White Star S.r.l.
Via Candido Sassone, 22/24
13100 Vercelli, Italia
www.whitestar.it

ISBN 88-8095-959-X
REPRINTS:
1 2 3 4 5 6   07 06 05 04 03

Printed in Italy by Officine
Grafiche De Agostini, Novara

CONTENTS

WHITE STAR
PUBLISHERS

Andalusia

1 The chimney of an underground dwelling peeps out in front of the white bell-tower of the Barrio Troglodita in Guadix where Andalusian prehistory mixes with the modern day.

2/7 Casares is a bright pueblo blanco perched on the Malaga hills. The gorgeous views from this isolated town in the middle of harsh countryside well repay the effort required to reach it.

3/6 This old print shows the cathedral and port of the sea town of Malaga. Its history is typical of other coastal towns in being linked to the events of the Mediterranean world. It was founded by the Phoenicians and was an important Arab port from the 8th century until the conclusion of the Reconquest when it passed into Catholic hands.

8 top The Puente de la Barqueta is only one of the many futuristic buildings constructed for Expo 1992, the international exhibition held in Seville. Five hundred years after the revolutionary "discovery" of America, the Andalusian city's international show reflected both the past and the future: it recalled the times when riches flowed into the city from across the ocean and looked to the future in more than 100 pavilions on the Isla de la Cartuja.

8-9 Plaza de España lies majestically in the center of Seville and is an important example of early 20th-century Spanish architecture. The impressive semi-circular building around it was the Spanish pavilion in the Ibero-American Exposition of 1929.

The most commonly held ideas of those who turn their attention to Andalusia for the first time can be summarized as sea, flamenco and bull-fighting. A land of great and unrivalled beauty, a triangle with softened edges that rears its head in the direction of Africa, Andalusia is not at all the fun-loving region where all women are the image of Carmen and all men Don Juan. Nor is it simply an immensely long strip of sandy coast crowded with hotels and 1980s-tourist attractions. It is not even the arid desert where only olive trees grow. In short, it is not the sum of the stereotypical images that began to spread around the world after the end of Franco's regime that often resulted in confusion between the representation of the whole of Spain and the real Andalusia.

For those who know and love this region, which over the centuries has seen its boundaries expand and shrink depending on which civilization ruled over it until they reached their present set, such superficiality of attitude is, to say the least, deserving of severe reprimand. Officially created an autonomous community in 1981, Andalusia is a land that, perhaps due to its geographic position, has been of fundamental importance to both European and world history. Lying at the extreme limit of the Mediterranean, its ports were favored

during antiquity; in the Middle Ages it was the theater of the great encounter/clash between Europeans and Africans and, shortly after, the trampoline that launched sailors and missionaries to the "discovery" of the New World. Having ventured into the difficult business of international power-broking, over the following centuries it first suffered the offences caused by English piracy (for long time told about), then those of Napoleon's forces against which the Spanish monarchy was unable to protect its kingdom. In the recent past, it has generously offered its resources to the strategic designs of the allied forces.

The identity of Andalusia is however a series of reflected images that has often been pillored. And yet, the southernmost tip of the Iberian peninsula is certainly a singular area if only for the way in which the inhabitants leave the final part of their words unsaid.

What, then, is it that Andalusia and Andalusians do not share with the rest of the world? History tells us that the region used to be much larger than it is today and also divided, above all during the period of Christian reconquest. Its modern-day inhabitants are the descendants of African, Italian, German and gypsy peoples, not to mention South American immigrants. A seemingly contradictory observation might reasonably suggest that

10 top Ayamonte is a tiny group of white buildings set in the tranquility of the Coto Doñana. Its dusty roads are half-deserted nearly all the year but at Pentecost they burst with pilgrims converging from all over Spain to worship the famous Virgen del Rocío.

it was in this very mixture that the kernel of "Andalusianness" lies: the secular amalgamation of so very different cultures in an ideal land, which fate has benignly overseen and encouraged. The reference to works of art, churches, Arab-style gardens, the paintings of Velázquez and the poetry of Góngora, illuminated Korans and enamelled *azulejos* is even too explicit and taken for granted. Nevertheless, it is in the creation of human works, which have been and continue to be so extraordinarily munificent in this region (the Nobel prize winner for Literature, Antonio Machado, is a perfect example), that we can see a valid element of the Andalusian identity.

10-11 The gentle hills of the countryside around the pueblo blanco *of Olvera in the province of Cadiz are typical of Andalusia. Long rows of silver olive trees stand out against the dark fields. The favorable climate has meant this area has always been an agricultural paradise.*

11 A fisherman prepares his nets for the next trip to sea in a peaceful sandy cove near to Nerja on the Costa del Sol. The towns on the Andalusian coast of the Mediterranean have been fishing ports and busy trading centers since ancient times.

On the other hand, it would be pure vanity to read the poignant poetry of Lorca and to claim to have sounded the Andalusian soul. The effort must be much more intense and involve all the senses. Sight is not enough to admire the gentle hills of Jerez lined with vines or the exaltations of Allah in plaster on the walls of the Alhambra. Touch is also necessary to perceive the thousand types of sand along the coast or the flank of an Arab horse; and hearing to appreciate the vibrant melodies of the *cante jondo* – the deep singing – or the shouts of festival crowds. Smell and taste are essential to savor the verdure of the *sierras*, the strawberries from Huelva, the flowers that nod on the patios, an aperitif with *tapa* (small mouthfuls to whet the appetite that always accompany a good drink) or a *gazpacho* (cold soup with tomatoes whisked with other raw vegetables).

This series of reflected images is, without doubt, the only way to understand what Andalusia really is: to walk through its streets and see oneself in the faces of the bearers of the statues in the Good Friday parade, in the vault of the cathedral that is also a mosque, in a tower built so that it was possible to mount a horse inside, in the sly glance of Velázquez seen behind the royal family in one of his most famous paintings, in the fountains with their infinite water spouts in the gardens of the Generalife, in the succulent tomatoes of Almeria. It is a series of reflections that makes an object, a person, a view or an animal evoke a thousand or more images, even when in complete contrast – like Expo '92 in Seville and the cave dwellers in Guadix. Andalusia – rich and cultured, poor and lively, hot and reserved: it is a series of reflections whose story began with the history

Alcazaba walls of Almeria

Olive trees in the surroundings of Baena

Horse-riders at the Seville Fair

Rock dwellings at Guadix near Granada

Palos de la Frontera

Huelva

Monasterio de la Rábida

Atlantic Ocean

Costa de la Luz

Lighthouse topping Cabo de Gata, Almeria

Gardens in the Alcázar of Cordoba

16-17 The unmistakable golden dome of the new cathedral of Cadiz gleams behind the colored houses along the Caleta, the section of the coast that joins the small island to the mainland.

18-19 The remains of the Arab fort of Antequera are tinged pink by the sunset. The lovely town north of Malaga has a large number of churches, the best-known being Santa María la Mayor.

Sierra Morena

Sierra Morena

Río Guadalquivir

Medina az Zarra
Almodóvar del Río
Cordoba

Ubeda
Baeza

Sierra de Segura

Jaén

Italica

Montilla
Cabra

Velez Blanco

Siville

Alcalá la Real

Baza

Rocío
Las Marismas

Guadix
Granada

Sierra de los Filabres

Antequera

Sierra Nevada

Jerez de la Frontera

Ronda

Mulhacén

Almeria

Río Guadalete

Serrania de Ronda

Malaga

Nerja

Las Alpujarras

Cadiz

Marbella

Cabo de Gata

Estepona

Costa del Sol

Cabo Trafalgar

Algeciras
Gibraltar

Tarifa

Strait of Gibraltar

Ceuta

Mediterranean Sea

Morocco

Melilla

20-21 Animals were also typical subjects of Iberian sculpture from the 7th to the 1st century BC. Lions were particularly popular, like the Lion of Baena in the picture. They were carved in high relief in the limestone with just enough essential features to characterize the animal precisely.

Andalusia is both young and old; young relatively speaking for its recent geological formation during the Tertiary period but old from an anthropological point of view as man has been present there since the middle Palaeolithic times. The bones found in Gibraltar, Játiva and Piñar are proof of the passage of Neanderthal man from Africa onto Andalusian territory. Other evidence, such as the megalithic remains in the provinces of Almeria and Malaga, are the traces left by the tribes generically named the Iberian peoples that later inhabited this area of the peninsula during Neolithic times from about 3000 BC. But it is

20 left The Lady of Baza, a sculpture housed at the Archeological Museum of Madrid, is an example of Iberian art that flourished along the Mediterranean coast of what is today

Andalusia. In this type of sculpture, women were usually dressed in a tunic that reached down to their feet and a cloak with hems that formed pleats. They are shown in a solemn pose.

21 top left This flute-player from the 1st century BC comes from Osuna near Seville. The work was carved in high relief and is one of the many of its kind found in this area of Andalusia where figures of warriors were also found.

with the Tartessos people that the history of human settlements in Andalusia becomes more interesting. The period and area in which they were present is still imprecisely defined but the fascination of their culture is incomparable. This is partly because the Tartessians were presumed to have arrived from a legendary land existing at the edge of the known world of that time, and partly for the excellent quality of the objects ascribed to them that have been found in the provinces of Huelva and Seville.

21 right This alabaster statuette is from Galera near Granada. The artistic influences of other Mediterranean cultures can be seen in its design; the Andalusian coasts were colonized by the Greeks and the Phoenicians and sculptures of sphinxes have been found nearby.

22 right This small bronze statue from the British Museum is a Tartessian work known as the Soldier of Medina de las Torres. The figure is wearing a head-dress very different to that of an Iberian soldier and he used to hold a weapon, now lost, in his closed and raised left fist.

22 left The Tartessian craftsmen were skillful in metalworking as shown by the objects found in the area where this "mythical" civilization flourished. This splendid vase with a stirrup handle ending in a mouth in the shape of a feline's head is an exquisite example.

22 center At Despegñaperros, where this statuette was found, a shrine has been found in a cave. Foot soldiers and cavalry, mainly forged in bronze, were often depicted in Iberian art.

These handmade objects forged of various materials act as a sort of identity card for the Tartessians who settled more or less in the southern part of the Guadalquivir valley. Besides their creative and technical skills, the Tartessians were recognized by other Mediterranean peoples as fine navigators and skilled traders that traveled as far as the north of the peninsula up both coasts and down to the south as far as the Canary Islands. The products they exchanged were mostly metals such as copper and tin from the rich mines around Huelva. Tartessos, the Iberian region that surrounded the European Pillar of Hercules, grew uninterruptedly until the 6th century BC when it reached its peak under Arganthonius. According to Greek sources Tartessos was considered a proper state, a fertile country as rich in fruit, vegetables and live-stock as in gold and silver.

At roughly the time of the existence of the Tartessians, several Indo-European peoples, of which the most representative is the Celts, migrated to the Iberian peninsula from central Europe and settled also in the extreme south.

They eventually merged with the native peoples to form the Celtiberians.

23 bottom left The horse rider in the picture is almost certainly a soldier and comes, like many others, from Despegñaperros. Besides being shown in warlike attitudes, horses were one of the most popular animals to be depicted in Iberian sculptures.

23 top right These magnificent long-stemmed gold candlesticks kept in the Archeological Museum of Madrid were found at Lebrija, near Seville. They are a fine example of the technical level reached by Iberian goldsmiths.

23

The Mediterranean coast was also populated by seafaring peoples such as the Phoenicians who, around 1100 BC established a production center at Gadir, modern-day Cadiz. The Phoenicians were followed by the Greeks and the Carthaginians who substantially altered the political balance of the Andalusian coasts and caused the inexorable decline of the flourishing Tartessian kingdom.

The Phocaean established a trading center at Mainake near Malaga, and the Carthaginians closed the western sea routes to all peoples after the battle of Alaila so giving themselves the monopoly on Andalusian trade. This situation brought about the dissolution of Tartessos, the exclusion of the Phoenicians and the reaction of the Romans who felt themselves threatened in the north of the Iberian peninsula (which they controlled) by the expansionist policy of the Carthaginians.

*24 top and 25 top
The gold necklace
pendant and fibula
are part of a set of
Phoenician jewellery
known as the
Carambolo Treasure.
They were discovered
in 1958 in Cerro del*
*Carambolo near
Camas as part of 21
items that are the
pride of the
Archeological
Museum of Seville for
the quality of their
manufacture and
material value.*

*24 bottom The
presence of
Phoenicians in
Andalusia has been
proven by abundant
finds ascribed to this
great sea-going
people. This bronze
figurine from the
Seville Archeological
Museum dates from
the 6th century BC
and probably
represents Astarte,
the Phoenician
goddess who was
mother of all the gods.*

*25 bottom This
Carthaginian
bronze-bodied
statuette with a gold
mask was found near
Cadiz. It dates from
between the 7th and
6th century BC and
may represent Ptah, a
deity that originated
in Egypt.*

Tension rose until the outbreak of the Second Punic War in 218 BC, which brought about the unchallenged dominance of the Romans over the Carthaginians in Spain. The decisive event took place in 209 BC when Publius Scipio took Carthago Nova in Spain (modernday Cartagena). By 206 BC, the Iberian peninsula, divided into Hispania Citerior in the north and Hispania Ulterior in the south, was already considered a Roman province. Nonetheless, the native races put up a certain resistance to the Roman troops, which were rendered less effective by internal divisions, for example, the rivalry between Julius Caesar and Pompey that led to the battle of Munda (Montilla) near Cordoba in 45 BC. When events brought greater stability, the renewal and reforming work

26 top left The contribution of Publius Cornelius Scipio, the young Roman commander, was of fundamental importance in the Second Punic War during which the victorious Roman army succeeded in chasing the Phoenicians out of the south of Iberia.

26 bottom right Rivalry between Julius Caesar and Pompey came to an end in what is today Andalusia. The two generals faced one another in 45 BC at Montilla (then known as Munda) near Cordoba in a famous battle that saw Caesar defeat his rival. The conflict marked the end of the internal struggles that had prevented the Romans from installing a real dominion in the southernmost strip of Iberia.

undertaken by the Romans knew no obstacles.

First, the peninsula was divided once more (27 BC) under Augustus (63 BC to 14 AD), this time into three provinces, and the Roman law was introduced. Hispania Ulterior was divided into Lusitania in the west, Baetica in the south, and Tarraconensis (the province that included the entire Hispania Citerior) in the

27 bottom Thanks to the legislative work of Augustus, Hispania Baetica was created when Hispania Ulteriore (or southern Hispania) was divided. The name was taken from the river that crossed it, the Baetis to the Romans, which is today called the Guadalquivir.

east. The borders of the southernmost province, Baetica (the name comes from *Baetis,* the Latin name for Guadalquivir) with the capital Corduba, enclosed most of what is today the autonomous Andalusian province except for a portion of modern-day Extremadura. Gades became the administrative center of northern Africa (Mauritania Tingitana).

26-27 The photograph shows the Lex Coloniae Genetive Giulie *(municipal law of Spain), issued by Julius Caesar in 44 BC. At the time, the peninsula was divided into Hispania Citerior and Hispania Ulterior. The latter was later subdivided into Lusitania, Baetica and part of Tarraconensis.*

27

It is no surprise that Baetica became one of the most flourishing provinces in the Roman empire; its strategic position, the climate suited to the production of wine and oil and its ancient fishing tradition were all factors that contributed to its development. This rich land soon became the natural setting for splendid cities founded by the Romans such as Italica (Santiaponce), Malaka (Malaga), or cities that were later expanded and enriched with monuments such as Hispalis (Seville). Roman domination brought reform of the agricultural system (which led to the formation of large estates), the introduction of new mining techniques at the gold mines in Cordoba and the

28 top Besides the Roman emperors Hadrian and Trajan, Andalusia was the birthplace of two important men of culture: Seneca the rhetorician and Lucius Anneus Seneca, both from Cordoba. The second, shown in the picture, was the son of the first.

28 bottom Hadrian was the second Roman emperor to come from Andalusia. This cultured lover of art and literature was born at Italica, today Santiaponce. It is said that when he first moved to Rome, he was only able to speak Latin with a strong Iberian pronunciation, which sounded very odd to the audiences of his first speeches.

28-29 Trajan is depicted with Sura in this detail from the Trajan Column in Rome. The emperor was born at Italica in 53 AD and left his homeland early but he returned "ideally" before his death when he indicated Hadrian as his successor.

silver mines in the Sierra Morena, the transformation of food products such as *garum* (the typical tasty sauce made from salted and fermented fish entrails) and introduction of the Roman legal system as well as magnificent architecture, sculpture and mosaic art.

At Italica, where the two great Roman emperors Trajan and Hadrian were born, the amphitheater and other superb ruins can still be admired as well as theaters (Malaga), aqueducts (Seville) and bridges (all over Andalusia). Some cities had huge populations for the time, like Cordoba with 35,000 inhabitants.

Roads were improved or built from nothing in accordance with a strictly functional plan for both military transfers and trading. In their almost 700 years of domination, the Romans turned Baetica into a beautiful and prosperous region – before the arrival of either the Barbarians or Arabs.

ΩΚΕΑΝΟС ΚΑΝΤΑΒΡΙΟС

ΑΥΤΙΚΟС ΩΚΕΑΝΟС

ΕΚΤΟС ΘΑΛΑССΑ:

ΙСΠΑΝΙΑ ΛΥ СΙΤΑΝΙ

ΙСΠΑΝΙΑ ΒΑΙ ΤΙΚΗ

ΙΒΗΡΙΚΟΝ ΠΕΛΑΓ

ΗΡΑΚΛΕΙ ΠΟΡΘΜΟС

of semi-abandonment and conditions were prepared for the most important invasion in Andalusian history.

The Caliphate of Damascus had extended his influence as far as Tangier the governor of which, Tariq ibn-Ziyad, crossed the strait in 711 and penetrated the Iberian peninsula. Mount Calpe, the large rock he first stepped on, was renamed Jebel Tariq ("the mountain of Tariq") an Arab name that was later transmuted into Gibraltar. The inevitable clash between the Arabs and the Visigoths under Roderick saw the defeat of the defenders and the advance of the invaders across the whole of the peninsula. The Arabs eventually dominated all of Iberia except for the Basque coun-

When the decline of Roman political life and the pressure of the Barbarians brought the collapse of the empire, provinces like Baetica also suffered the break-up of the system it had been so cosseted by and it was soon invaded and conquered.

The first to do so were the Vandals; they crossed the Pyrenees, traveled south and then continued into Africa across the strait (in 429) from Julia Traducta (the city of Tarifa). This short passage was responsible for the most symbolic of marks Andalusia still keeps: it is supposed that Julia Traducta was renamed *Portu*

Vandalu, which was gradually turned into Wandalus, the name that the Arabs, by placing the article *al* in front, called the ancient province of Baetica *al-Andalus*.

Without meeting any great resistance, another barbarous people from central Europe, the Visigoths, founded a kingdom in Andalusia and removed the old Hispanic-Roman ruling class from power. Nevertheless, unable to maintain control, the new central authority that Andalusia depended on, which had settled in Toledo, was progressively weakened. These territories were left in a state

try. However there were divisions within the ranks of the invaders who were not all Arabs but partly Berber. The first Arab wave led by Tariq were Berber soldiers captained by Arab or Syrian commanders whereas the second, led by Musa one year later, was a force of oriental soldiers. In the end, the Umayyad dynasty of Cordoba took control and unified al-Andalus. This came about following the flight of Umayyad Prince Abd ar-Rahman I to the south of Spain via Almuñecar. By shifting alliances and using mercenary support, he placed himself in a position of power, attacking and defeating all his opponents until 756 when he established himself as Emir after his last victory near Cadiz.

30 top This map taken from Claudius Ptolomeus Geographicorum Libri *shows the Iberian peninsula when it was still under Arab domination.*

30-31 Islamic domination of Spain, particularly in Andalusia, prompted an amazing artistic output. This plate from Malaga has a typical polychrome decoration of floral motifs predominantly in blue and ochre.

31 This hunting scene is a striking bas-relief carved during the times of the Moslem Fatimid dynasty. The Fatimids dominated much of northern Africa inhabited by Berber-Arab peoples.

This was the start of a historical period for all of Iberia but especially for Andalusia. Its influence was felt for centuries in all fields of daily life and in every branch of culture, art and science. Today, the remains of Arab rule are the most fascinating traces of Andalusia's past.

The fundamental characteristic of Arab dominion in Spain was religious tolerance whereby the Christians and Jews were allowed to practise their faiths. If this appears a symptom of advanced civilization and superior culture, it also had economic interests. If the followers of the other two great monotheist religions had been constrained to convert to Islam, they would automatically not have been obliged to pay taxes. As they made up by far the largest part of the workforce, it was clearly in the Arab interest to allow them to continue with their occupations.

As time passed, the Arabs mixed with the indigenous population so blurring the lines between the different peoples.

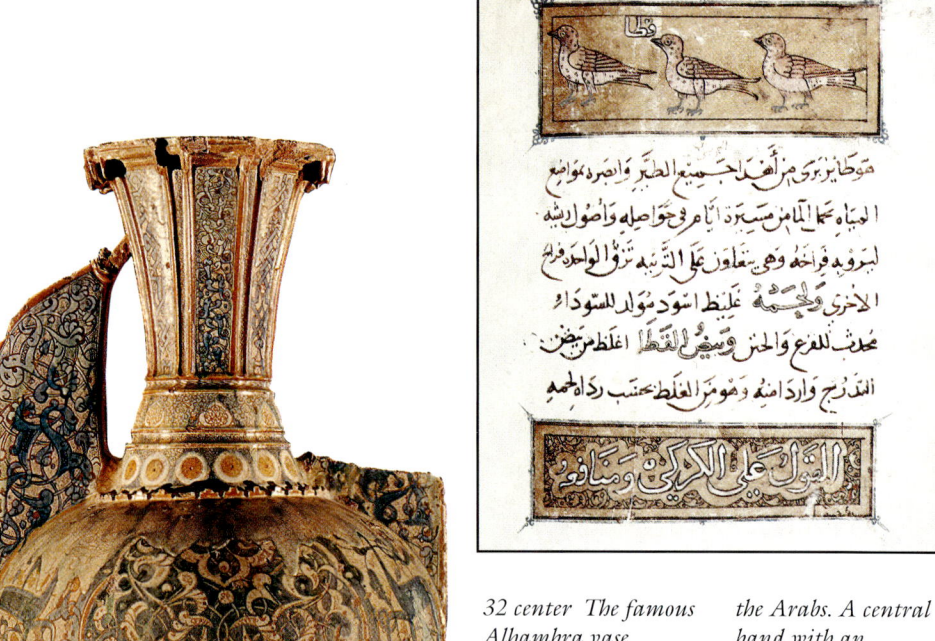

32 center The famous Alhambra vase probably dates from the 14th century. It is one of the loveliest examples of painted pottery produced by the Arabs. A central band with an inscription passes between the floral decorations on a cobalt blue background.

32 bottom left This bronze deer comes from Medina Azahara. It is one of the many examples of the Arabs' metalworking skill produced throughout Andalusia.

The political, administrative and religious capital of al-Andalus was Cordoba, a splendid city that reached its peak under the Moslem dominion. Even today, the glory of the Arab capital can be recognized in the city's ancient center although time and modern life have erased some of its magic.

As had occurred to Baetica under the Romans, Andalusia disclosed its riches to the Moors. The products of a flourishing agriculture and the metals from its mines contributed to providing al-Andalus with an enviable economy. The Arabs imported many plants and vegetables, the modern names of which betray their origin – *alcachofa* (artichoke), *azafrán* (saffron) and *algodón* (cotton).

The Arab love for parks and botanical gardens is shown in the archetypal Generalife gardens in Granada. They used their advanced engineering knowledge to adapt ancient water systems built by the Romans for irrigation purposes.

The consolidation of al-Andalus power, splendor and prestige was especially carried out by the Caliph Abd ar-Rahman III, but after his death a slow but irreversible slide towards disintegration set in.

32 right The Arabs handed down huge amounts of manuscripts and drawings dealing with the natural sciences as well as with chemistry and mathematics, subjects on which they were extraordinarily knowledgeable.

32-33 The vault of one of the three alcoves in the Room of the Kings in the Alhambra in Granada is the setting for this fresco that shows human figures which was forbidden by the Koran, therefore it was probably painted by Christian artists.

33 top Taken from Alfonso X's manuscript The Book of Games, the illustration shows two Arabs playing chess, a refined pastime that reached Andalusia with the arrival of the Arabs.

34 *This 14th-century miniature from the* Chronicle of Spain *shows Rodrigo Diaz de Bivar, the Cid Campeador, killing Martin Gomez. El Cid was a legendary figure of the medieval Catholics; he was the hero of the Reconquest and the scourge of the Arabs.*

The last powerful leader able to keep the Christian threat from the north at bay was al-Mansur. Although he was not a direct heir of the reigning dynasty, he obtained power through a series of stratagems. His bravery and ability stemmed the Christian invasion and held off the disintegration of al-Andalus for a while. Following al-Mansur, various figures occupied the throne of Cordoba but internal tensions and the massive presence of the Berbers in revolt ended in the dissolution of the Caliphate, which was officially decreed at Cordoba in 1031 by a council of ministers. The result was the creation of about 30 *reinos de taifa*, i.e., party kingdoms, some ruled by Berbers, such as Granada and Malaga, others by Moslems, like Cordoba and Seville.

The fragility created by the division of al-Andalus into small entities was the intrinsic factor that, coupled

35 bottom left The portrait is of Alfonso VI, king of Castile and León, who succeeded in advancing the threatening Catholic army south in the 11th century.

35 top right The Arabs were excellent horsemen and courageous soldiers; they put up a strenuous resistance to the Christian forces that slowly advanced south during the Reconquest.

ADEFONS: REX:PATER: PATRIE:

with the new wave of Christian enthusiasm, removed the final obstacles to the overrunning and destruction of al-Andalus as an entity. This was the period in which the dashing figure of El Cid Campeador took the stage: he was a hero to the Spaniards but a symbol of destruction to the Moors.

The architect of the reconquest of Islamic Spain during this period was Alfonso VI of Castile and León, a kingdom in the north of the country that was to become more and more important. Alfonso did not delay in sending his troops south until they reached Seville, then in the hands of the Abbasids headed by al-Mu'tamid. A counter-offensive was quickly launched supported by the Almoravid dynasty, Moslem integralists sent especially from Africa, and al-Mu'tamid defeated Alfonso at Sagrajas, near the city of Badajoz in Extremadura. The situation degenerated with the rise in rivalry between the Almoravids and al-Mu'tamid, which ended with the incumbent being dethroned by his "allies".

The Almoravids set up a regime based strictly on the *Koran* and al-Mu'tamid and his court were exiled. It seemed as though the determination of the Almoravids and their

36 top Alfonso X, "the Wise", appears in a miniature from a manuscript from the end of the 13th century. The king is remembered for the boost he gave to culture by welcoming men of science and literature (not only Christians) to his court and having Islamic and Hebrew texts translated.

36 bottom The turning point of the Reconquest took place in 1212 in Andalusia with the battle of Las Navas de Tolosa. Crusaders and Almohad "infidels" clashed in a bloody battle, which resulted in a victory for the Christians.

37 This beautifully made Moslem standard became the symbol of the Catholic victory at Las Navas de Tolosa.

unbending regime could withstand all pressure but events on the other side of the strait brought about the first signs of weakness.

Between 1145-1171, the Almohad dynasty opposed the Almoravids in northern Africa and later in Spain, following the Almoravid victories in al-Andalus. These new preachers of Islam differed from their predecessors by their more liberal interpretation of the *Koran*. The *taifa* of al-Andalus soon fell to the Almohads under Abu-Ya qub Yusuf who became caliph. With the arrival of these new conquerors, the ferocious defence of al-Andalus against the Christian forces trying in every way to win back the whole of the Iberian peninsula did not weaken. In 1211, the entire Christian world supported the cause of the northern Iberian kings following the proclamation of a crusade against the Arabs by Pope Innocent III. The Christian offensive culminated in the battle of Las Navas de Tolosa where the strategically positioned Mohammed al-Nasir, the new Arab leader, was crushed by the Christian forces led by Alfonso VII of Castile. The end of al-Andalus as an Arab political and military dominion was almost over. From then on, the kingdoms of Aragon and Castile competed to wipe out the last Arab resistance as, one by one, the Andalusian strongholds fell. Although surrounded by newly won back lands, Granada remained uncaptured and resisted for two more centuries before surrendering. During that time, Christian rule over the Moors showed a certain tolerance because the new governors recognized that it was to their benefit to assimilate the high levels of culture and art of the Andalusians rather than destroy them. And of course it was now possible for the Christians to tax the Arabs. It is in this atmosphere that the figure of Alfonso X "*el sabio*" (the Wise), king of Castile, stood out. This learned monarch boosted culture and the translating of many Arab texts.

The lands won back were slowly reoccupied and distributed among those who had distinguished themselves in battle against the Moors. The structure of Andalusian society was altered with the new estate owners at the top and unconverted Moslem workers and craftsmen and Jewish traders at the bottom. Such professions had no merits in the eyes of the Christians who boasted the purity of their blood, *"la limpieza de sangre"*, and many "gentlemen" who fell on hard times preferred to fight as mercenaries than take up professions that may have been dignified but not considered worthy of Christians.

38 top The painting shows the expulsion of the Arabs from Spain. The religious policy inaugurated by the "reyes católicos" "as strongly intransigent.

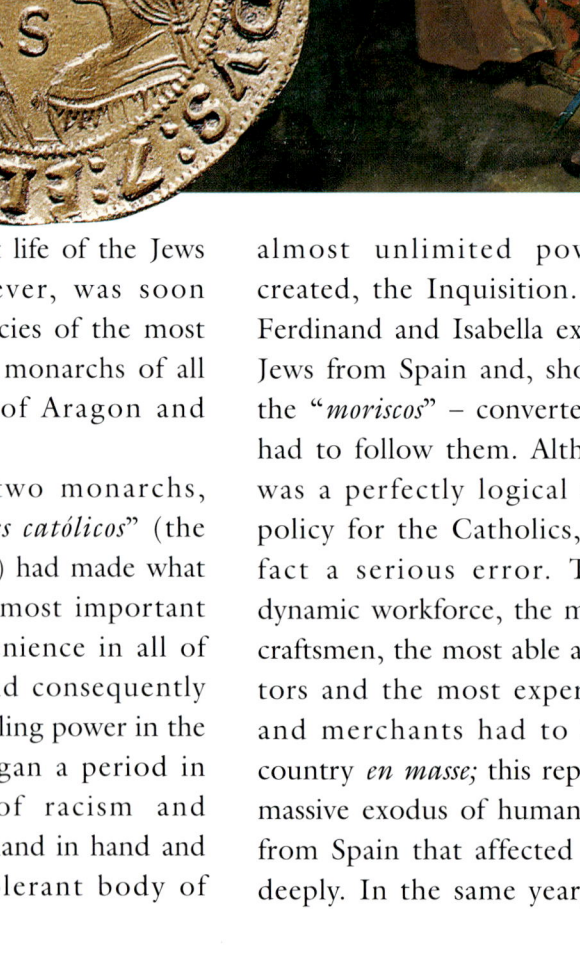

The relatively quiet life of the Jews and Arabs, however, was soon shaken by the policies of the most intolerant Spanish monarchs of all time, Ferdinand of Aragon and Isabella of Castile.

In 1479, these two monarchs, known as *"los reyes católicos"* (the Catholic Monarchs) had made what was probably the most important marriage of convenience in all of Spain's history and consequently become the controlling power in the country. They began a period in which policies of racism and Catholicism went hand in hand and a despicably intolerant body of

almost unlimited powers was created, the Inquisition. In 1492, Ferdinand and Isabella expelled the Jews from Spain and, shortly after, the *"moriscos"* – converted Arabs – had to follow them. Although this was a perfectly logical and ideal policy for the Catholics, it was in fact a serious error. The most dynamic workforce, the most skilful craftsmen, the most able administrators and the most expert doctors and merchants had to leave the country *en masse;* this represented a massive exodus of human resources from Spain that affected Andalusia deeply. In the same year, Granada

38 center This gold coin shows Isabella of Castile and Ferdinand of Aragon, the monarchs that completed the Reconquest.

38 bottom Christopher Columbus received permission to undertake his extraordinary voyage with a royal document, the Capitulaciones de Santa Fe, *signed in Granada during the last days of the siege.*

38-39 This 1890 painting depicts the surrender of the city of Granada. Amongst the crowd in the foreground we see the "reyes católicos" pointing at the city and the Alhambra.

39 bottom Included in the many historical episodes narrated in the azulejos *in Plaza de España is the surrender of the Arabs in Malaga, the important port on the Mediterranean closely associated with Granada.*

fell. The Moslem enclave that also included Malaga and Ronda had managed to survive thanks to a complex game of alliances and submissions played with the Catholic monarchs of the peninsula, but the domestic conflicts and policies of Ferdinand and Isabella, who had threatened the Alhambra and its occupants for more than 10 years, annihilated the last bastion of what had been the glorious caliphate of al-Andalus.

A modern era began for Andalusia closely linked to the most revolutionary journey that a reigning house had ever sponsored.

40 top Certain of
finding a new route
to the Indies across the
Atlantic Ocean, the
famous Genoan
navigator,
Christopher
Columbus, decided to
press his cause with
the Spanish Crown.

40 center The
realization of
Columbus's dream
came much closer on
17 April 1492 when
he received
authorization from
the "reyes católicos"
to set sail for the
Indies by a new
route.

40 bottom The
picture reproduces one
of the many
interpretations of
Columbus's
adventurous
transatlantic trip.
The three famous
ships, the Niña, the
Pinta and the Santa
Maria, unfurl their
sails unaware on their
way to the New
World.

41 This painting in
the Monasterio de la
Rábida, where
Columbus spent a
long period in
retreat, shows his
departure from Palos
de la Frontera near
Huelva. Columbus
and his crew weighed
anchor on 3 August
1492 and reached the
Bahamas in October
of the same year.

In 1492, Christopher Columbus set off from Palos de la Frontera in Andalusia west towards the Indies with Queen Isabella's blessing. From there it was but a short step to the land of the New World.

Many adventurers followed the route of the Andalusian crews of the Spanish caravels to the rich American lands.

Now that the prestige of Cordoba had vanished and Granada had fallen, it was the turn of Seville to become famous.

Queen Isabella set up the *"Casa de Contratación"* in the city, an institute responsible for everything that concerned the relations between Spain and its overseas colonies: trade, missions and administration

of justice and resources. Seville held the monopoly on this traffic and saw gold, silver and precious stones arrive in its port in great quantities, not to mention foodstuffs that had never been seen before like cocoa beans, potatoes and maize. Exports like textiles, oil and wine were equally profitable. Shortly after Cadiz also specialized in trade with the Americas given its favorable position on safer routes, but soon the idyllic situation of Andalusia's coasts would be threatened by the frequent and violent attacks of English piracy.

The attempts to keep the precious cargoes from the colonies safe had little effect: the convoys escorted by heavily armed galleons were plundered anyway by the "vassal" pirates of Her Majesty, Queen Elizabeth of England.

The effects of Philip II's short-sighted determination to annihilate the English sea-power with a single blow from his invincible Armada were felt fully in Andalusia. In 1587, Sir Francis Drake attacked and destroyed provisions and arms meant for the Armada in the port of Cadiz before it was able to head for Albion. The following year, the

42 center This engraving depicts the conquest of Cadiz by the powerful Dutch and English fleet in 1598. The city was sacked by the allied ships commanded by the Duke of Essex and Admiral Howard.

42 bottom Philip II of Spain was a centralizing monarch and fervent Catholic. He tried to oppose the ascending English power with the Armada but all his efforts were soundly trounced.

42 top left Sir Francis Drake, faithful subject of Queen Elizabeth of England, scourged the Andalusian coasts for years on piratical missions. Not only was he able to inflict heavy losses on Spanish trade with its colonies, he also played a fundamental role in the defeat of the "Invincible Armada" of Philip II.

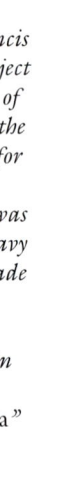

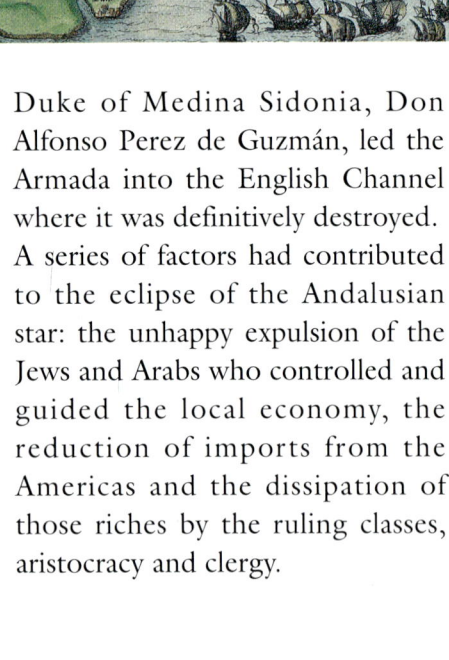

Duke of Medina Sidonia, Don Alfonso Perez de Guzmán, led the Armada into the English Channel where it was definitively destroyed. A series of factors had contributed to the eclipse of the Andalusian star: the unhappy expulsion of the Jews and Arabs who controlled and guided the local economy, the reduction of imports from the Americas and the dissipation of those riches by the ruling classes, aristocracy and clergy.

42-43 *This 17th-century print shows the aspect of the galleons: they were four-master military sail-ships fitted out to transport valuable merchandise from the colonies. The ship's guns were used for defense against acts of piracy.*

43 top *The crew of the Golden Hind, Sir Francis Drake's ship, prepares to board yet another Spanish galleon. Terrible stories have now been told for centuries in Andalusia about the English pirate.*

Galeon castellano.

RENACIMIENTO.

GALEONES DEL SIGLO XVII. SEGUN GRABADOS
pinturas, dibujos y descripciones de la
época.

On the other hand, as for the rest of the peninsula, this was one of the richest periods in history for Andalusian art and culture. The *Siglo de Oro*, or "Golden Century" that lasted over a century saw the birth of the Seville school of painting. This manner of painting was distinguished by the touch of realism and its most important exponents were Francisco de Zurbarán (1598-1664), Bartolomé Esteban Murillo (1618-1682) and the famous Diego Rodríguez de Silva y Velázquez (1599-1660). In the field of literature, the most symbolic writer was the Cordoban, Luis de Góngora y Argote (1561-1627), the Baroque poet with a unique style who wrote both simple and popular poetry as well as complex and difficult poems such as Soledades – "Solitudes".

44 Las Meninas *is one of Diego de Silva y Velázquez's most famous paintings and is a wonderful example of the Andalusian master's expertise. Originally trained in the city of* his birth, Seville, he later traveled to Madrid and Italy. His skill, thanks to which he is considered the innovator of realism in painting, brought him the post of Court painter.

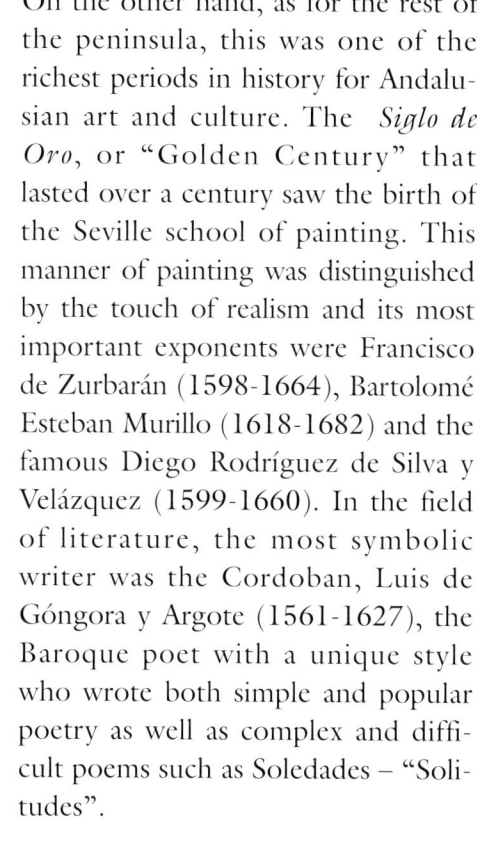

45 top The characteristic feature of the work of Bartolomé Esteban Murillo, Sevillan painter of the Siglo de Oro, *is the gentleness of the faces of his subjects, as seen in this picture* Sagrada Familia del pajarito.

45 center San Hugo en el Refectorio *is a painting by Francisco de Zurbarán, an artist of the Seville school who concentrated mainly on religious subjects. The painting is kept in the Museum of Fine Arts in Seville.*

45 bottom The inimitable touch of Velázquez distinguishes this portrait of one of Spain's greatest poets of all time, the Cordoban Luis de Góngora y Argote. The most important of Andalusian poets during the Siglo de Oro, Gongora *wrote verses characterized by lexical innovation and musicality. Among his best-known works are the* Soledades *and the poem* Polifemo y Galatea.

Andalusia suffered a sort of territorial expropriation in the wake of the decline of Spanish colonial power at the beginning of the 18th century. The Treaty of Utrecht brought the War of Succession to a definitive conclusion but it decided that Gibraltar was to be ceded to Britain. This situation, created in 1713 and still unchanged, was like a wound that has caused a light but unending pain in the hearts of the Spanish.

Following a period of relative calm, the beginning of the 19th century

saw the umpteenth invasion of Andalusia during the last act of Napoleon's irruption in the peninsula.

In the first weeks of 1810, the entire country except for Cadiz fell into the hands of the French. The Andalusian city, which stands on an island, was the last stronghold of the Spanish. Here the *cortes* was established, a parliament that enacted a liberal constitution as the first step towards a truly modern state. In reality, the French supremacy was never total in the extreme south of Spain. Soon Napoleon's men were eliminated thanks to the help of the English who supported the Spanish in this case, but the liberal constitution was returned to where it had come from when Ferdinand VII imposed a monarchy on the country.

This was the signal for a long period of internal struggle between the supporters of royal authority and those of the constitution.

47 bottom The famous constitution of Cadiz in 1812 was declared by the cortes while the city resisted the siege of Napoleon's forces. The picture shows the first page of the document, which depicts the city's defensive walls below the heading.

In this air of revolt, Andalusia showed itself to be a historical nerve point of anarchic and Marxist agitation. An example is the Mano Negra, an attempt at subversion of the ruling social class by a group of anarchists executed at Cadiz.

During the three-year Bolshevik period, 1918 to 1921, Andalusia was the scene of social clashes and peasant protests demanding rights from the estate owners for whom they worked. In just a short space of time, the PSOE, the Spanish socialist party, grew enormously in Andalusia although soon after,

from 1921 to 1923, it saw an equally spectacular loss of members.

Meanwhile, the problems associated with relations between traditional estate owners and their workers remained unresolved.

The year 1923 brought a coup d'état signalling the beginning of the dictatorship of Primo de Rivera, which lasted until 1929.

The increasingly fast turnaround of events overwhelmed all of Spain, and Andalusia found itself ruled by transition governments as it moved from democracy through the difficult years towards the outbreak of the Civil War after victory by the left in the 1936 elections.

In August of that year, Cordoba, Seville, Huelva, Cadiz and Granada rebelled whereas Jaén, Almeria and

Malaga remained faithful to the republic. Given that it was traditional for the people to support the left, fighting was extreme before the army could take control of the Andalusian provinces.

Against this historical background of violence and civil conflict, an episode of momentous impact took place – the assassination of poet Federico García Lorca. Lorca was a singer from Andalusia erroneously considered implicated in political events on the basis of his signature against Nazism. Today his assassination is remembered as one of the most tragic pages in the history of Andalusia, but the killing was symbolic of the climate of those years.

After the army of Queipo de Llano passed through Andalusia from Morocco to give support to the rebels in Madrid, the focal point of

the Civil War moved to the capital, and in 1939 the conflict ended with the victory of General Francisco Franco Bahamonde and the beginning of the age of Spanish dictatorship. Since the end of the Franco regime, Andalusia has for the most part followed the political developments of Spain. It has found itself in a middle position between the extremism of the supporters of Basque and Catalan independence and the widespread feeling of national unity. In 1981, a parliamentary resolution made Andalusia an Autonomous Community giving the region its own statute and administrative prerogatives "...como expresión de su identidad histórica..." (... as an expression of its historical identity ...).

50 top left *The white buildings of Tarifa, reminiscent of Africa, mark the southernmost point of Andalusia and Europe. Today it is a surfing paradise; in the past it was the "bridge" that the Arabs crossed from the other side of the strait.*

50 center left The crystalline waves of the Atlantic break on the long sandbars of Zahara de los Atunes, on the Costa de la Luz, south of Cabo de Trafalgar.

50 bottom left Luxuriant Mediterranean vegetation frames the wonderful little coves near Nerja on the Costa del Sol.

50 right The beaches of Cabo Roche wind around Conil de la Frontera, a fishing village north of Cabo de Trafalgar on the Costa de la Luz. These are picturesque and quiet corners far from the rush of the other seaside resorts: here, silence and the ocean are the main features.

*I*f one enters Andalusia from the south as the Arabs did in 711, one finds an independent territory on the first strip of land encountered where, ironically, the English language is spoken: Gibraltar. What used to be known as the Jebel Tariq (Mountain of Tariq) is a huge granite massif with an unmistakable shape. Facing out over the Bay of Algeciras, its slant seems to make it want to pursue Tarifa Point towards Africa. Tarifa is the southernmost urban settlement in Andalusia and the historical port of the Strait of Gibraltar. It divides the coast of southern Spain into two parts, the Costa de la Luz (coast of light) on the Atlantic side to the west and the Costa del Sol (coast of the sun) on the Mediterranean to the east.

50-51 From the top of the Rock, over 1250 feet high, there is a splendid view of Gibraltar, the tiny British dominion inside Andalusian territory. This rock is joined to the mainland by a narrow isthmus less than 1000 yards wide.

51 top
The unmistakable silhouette of the Peñón de Gibraltar (the name given by the Spanish to the Rock) is reflected in the clear waters of the bay of Algeciras.

*52 left The source of
the Guadalquivir is
in the Sirra de
Segura in the north-
east of Andalusia.
The river is one of the
longest in the Iberian
peninsula and flows
406 miles to San
Lucar de Barrameda
where it reaches the
Atlantic.*

*52 top The many and
varied types of fauna
in the Coto Doñana
include large
populations of roe
and fallow deer.*

*52-53 A huge variety
of environments can
be found inside the
Coto Doñana: the
marismas (seaside
marshland) with wild
horses are a typical
feature.*

The Costa de la Luz is a continuous chain of beaches and cliffs that follow one another towards the border with Portugal. A little to the north of Cadiz, Andalusia's largest river, the Guadalquivir, flows into the sea. The river has its source in the Sierra de Segura, the mountainous north-ern tip of the region, then flows through Cordoba and Seville before reaching the sea. Its course gives rise to one of Spain's most spectacular landscapes. The marshy, green river basin makes an ideal habitat for many species, particularly birds. The marvelous and varied fauna that

53 top Flamingoes (Phoenicopterus ruber) live happily in certain parts of the nature park at Coto Doñana. They are just one of the many bird species to be seen in this protected area.

53 center and bottom In terms of size and variety, the bird-life in Coto Doñana is one of the greatest in Europe both for permanent residents and migrating birds. Lovers of wet-lands,

birds like the moorhen (Gallinula chloropus) – in the center picture – and the widgeon (Netta rufina) – in the bottom picture – find the Coto Doñana their ideal habitat.

populate the marshes of the Guadalquivir, the pines and the adjacent strip of beach all fall within the Parque Nacional de Doñana, the largest protected area in the Iberian peninsula. It is home to more than 200 species of plants typical of the Mediterranean and north African environments. Roe deer, fallow deer, lynx and golden eagles are to be found in this wild and undisturbed area as well as reptiles, herons, amphibians and spoonbills.

54 top Dozens of rows of vines process over the gentle hills around Jerez de la Frontera. The wine of Jerez is known across the world as sherry and has been produced since time immemorial in this area blessed by a favorable climate and suitable characteristics of the land.

54 center The wine of Jerez is obtained from a mixture of Palomino, Moscatelle and Tintilla grapes, which are harvested in September, left to dry in the sun and then pressed separately. After a suitable aging period, the wine is ready for tasting. The characteristics of the taste depend for the most part on the length of the aging period. The color of younger wines is pale and the aroma is delicate while older wines are more intense, have a higher alcohol content and are amber in color.

54 bottom At the time of the Romans, Jerez wine was exported around the empire in clay amphoras. Today the wine can be drunk after drawing it off from traditional terracotta containers.

To the east and south of Doñana (which mostly lies within the province of Seville) there are a number of large and small towns that conserve a sense of the most epic chapter of Spain's history in their names: Morón de la Frontera, Arcos de la Frontera and Jerez de la Frontera are the best known names that once signalled the dividing line between the territory under Arab control and the zone slowly reconquered by the Christian forces during the reconquest.

Jerez is a sort of capital of this whole area. Since time immemorial its land has been marked by vines used to produce Jerez, the perfumed wine that Sir Francis Drake, the popular English pirate, took home in quantity and introduced to England with the name of sherry.

The countryside here is sinuous and gentle, lined with rows of green vines that contrast with the warm colors behind.

Another wine, this time sweet and very alcoholic, competes with Jerez for the top wine spot.

It is made from the nectar in the vines behind Malaga, one of Andalusia's largest cities, that overlooks the Costa del Sol.

The wines made here are a raisin wine to be drunk with desserts and a red suitable for strong tasting foods.

54-55 Signatures, emblems, phrases and poetic verses distinguish the barrels held in the bodegas, the cellars where Jerez is made. Many families of Anglo-Saxon origin left their homes in the past to settle down in this corner of Andalusia and produce the wine so appreciated by Sir Francis Drake.

55 top Maturation of Jerez is a delicate process that requires the positioning of several levels of communicating barrels on top of one another so that the wine runs down as it slowly passes through the various stages of aging.

56 top As unexpected oases in the desert, marvelous golf courses are located around Marbella, the famous beach resort that is the symbol of the Costa del Sol.

56-57 Estepona combines the attraction of its original Arab city with the bustle of a modern seaside tourist resort. Situated just north of Gibraltar on the Costa del Sol, it has preserved its characteristic old city center despite the assault of tourism.

Over the past few decades, Malaga and its surrounding area has risen to become a top tourist destination and achieve world renown.

With a few exceptions, the province's coastline offers a sort of perfect tourist industry able to offer art, natural areas of great beauty, modern and efficient infrastructures and entertainment for any sort of holiday. Centers such as Torremolinos, Marbella and Estepona no longer need to advertise themselves, such is their fame. Once away from the crowded sandy beaches, tall modern hotels and thousands of new attractions like the golf courses, this area has surprises in store. For example, Malaga can be seen by visiting the places where Picasso, who was born here, started his career. Estepona, which was founded by the Phoenicians, still has the fascinating atmosphere bequeathed to it by the Arabs. Leaving this former fishing village, the passage inland does not seem so sudden: the eye of the visitor is gradually presented with fewer crowds and a greater extent of wild nature.

58 top The Grazalema Nature Park was created in 1984 to protect the calcareous geological environment and the flora, including a rare species of fir tree, that are typical of the area. The fauna is typical of mountain areas and has a sizeable number of birds, especially birds of prey.

58 bottom Grazalema is an enchanting village that clings to the slopes of the Sierra de Grazalema. Its houses are a splash of white against the green of the surrounding vegetation. The abundant rain the area receives has encouraged a wide variety of plant life to grow.

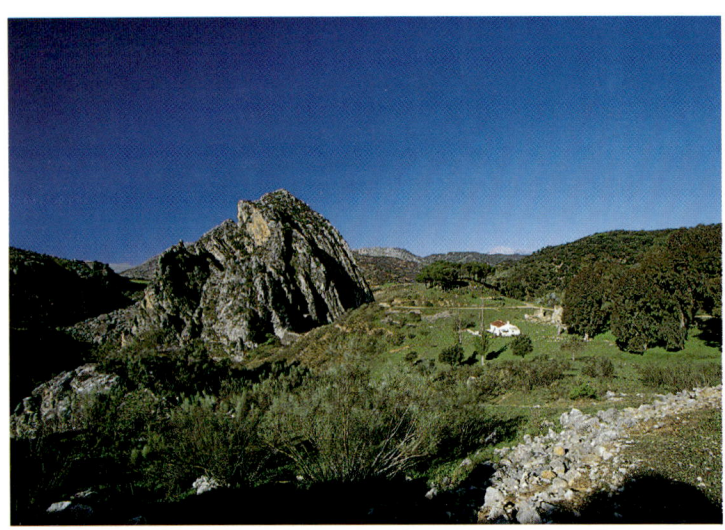

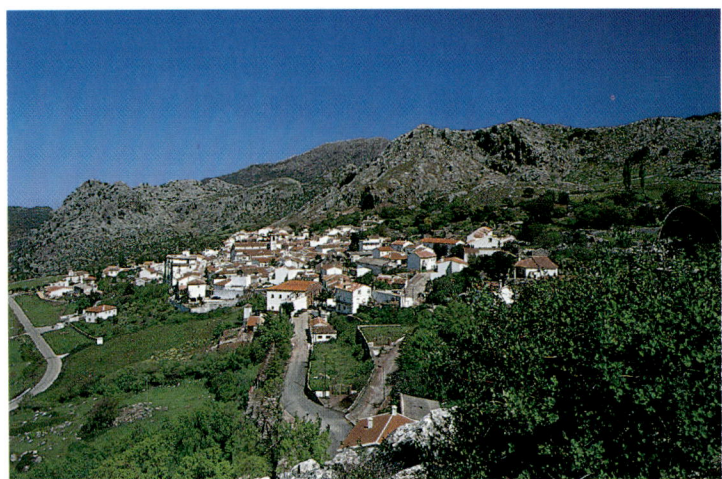

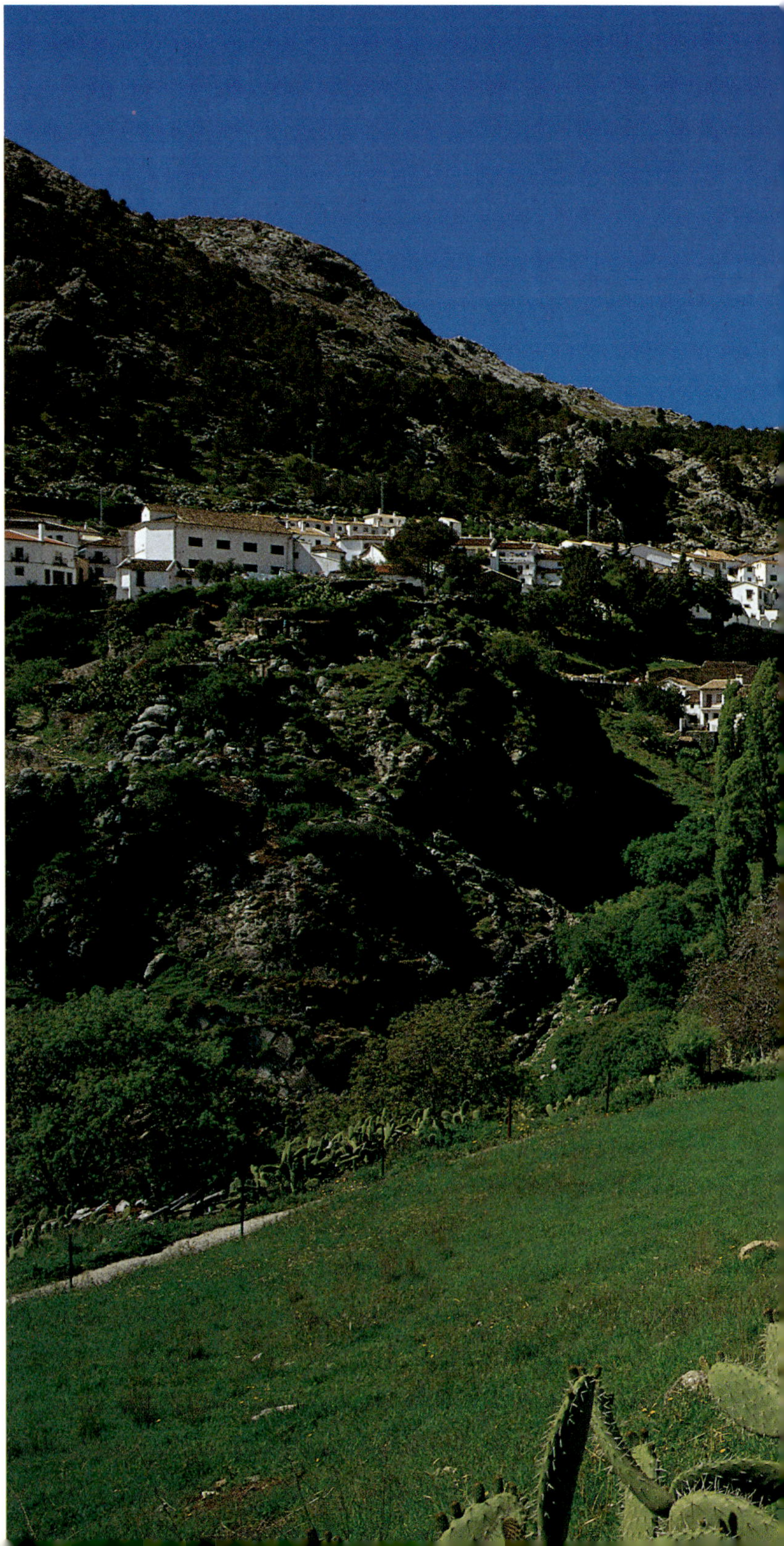

58-59 Grazalema Nature Park stretches east of the province of Cadiz. The reserve is famous for its interesting varieties of fauna and many species of trees.

A little further north along the boundary between the provinces of Cadiz and Malaga, the countryside changes again.
Tranquillity and history prevail and unexpected treasures like the pale-colored Ronda appear in the lovely Sierra de Grezalema, with its amazing bridge that spans the Guadalevin ravine, or the caves of Cueva de la Pileta with prehistoric wall paintings.

59 top Ronda is certainly one of the most spectacular inland localities in the province of Malaga. The two parts of Ronda on the hills of the Serrania de Ronda – the Arab "Ciudad" and "Mercadillo" – are joined by the famous Ponte Nuevo.

From here to the white cities, appearing as dazzling white stains painted on the hills, the road is short but twisty. There are in fact many more than a dozen *pueblos blancos*, which are found mainly between Ronda and Antequera. The best known among them are Casares and Gaucín, but they also include Medina Sidonia near Cadiz. Moreover, Medina Sidonia reminds one of the historic deeds that had involved the dukes of the same name.

60 top Olvera is one of the largest of the pueblos blancos. It is not simply the color of the buildings that makes Olvera interesting; in the center of the dazzling whiteness stands a Renaissance church and an Arab fort that seem to oppose one another just as their respective builders did in the past.

60-61 Casares is the most well-known of the pueblos blancos, a series of white centers built on the dark rocks of the Malaga hills. The remains of a warm colored church rise from the highest point of Casares. From here, the view stretches to the horizon over the wild and natural surroundings.

61 top Setenil, located near Ronda and almost set in the rock, is one of the smallest pueblos blancos.

61 bottom The last light of the day tinges the sky over Medina Sidonia pink to create a pretty contrast with the white buildings. The town is built on a rise in the middle of the zone of La Frontera and is one of those collectively named pueblos blancos.

Going east along the Costa del Sol towards the eastern border of Andalusia, one reaches the provinces of Granada and Almeria, each of which discloses its wildly contrasting landscapes.

Having passed the coastal villages of Almuñecar and Motril, the level of the land begins to rise until it culminates in Monte Mulhacén, the highest peak in the peninsula. At 11,424 feet high, it towers over the Sierra Nevada, the mountain chain that dominates Granada making one forget that this is one of the driest and hottest regions of Europe.

North of the mountain range stretch vast plateaus, interrupted here and there by low hills covered with olive trees. Lovely views are to be seen, including that of the massive castle of Lalacalahorra, which stands out against the Sierra.

The mountains of Granada are distinguished by two very different panoramas: on one side there are the modern ski facilities used in the 1996 World Skiing Championships, and on the other, the Guadalfeo and its tributaries flow among the rocks creating almost Nordic scenes.

Further south, tiny villages cling to the rocks of the Alpujarras, harsh mountains where strong resistance was put up by the Arabs who had escaped from Granada at the time of Philip II.

63 bottom
The Sierra Nevada takes its name from the permanent snow caps of the mountains. The mountain range is home to Spain's highest mountain, Mount Mulhacén, at 11,424 feet high. The modern facilities make the pistes of the Sierra Nevada a great attraction for winter sports lovers. In 1996, these mountains were the site of the World Ski Championships.

64 top This is the coast near the picturesque fishing village of Las Negras, just a stone's throw from Cabo de Gata. The sand is dark-colored where the land meets the sea.

64-65 The coast away from the tourist resorts on the Costa del Sol is a continual surprise. The isolated and empty beaches of the blue Mediterranean are a joy to be discovered.

Once the pistes of Solynieve in the Sierra Nevada and the harshness of Las Alpujarras have been left behind, one enters the provincial territory of Almeria.

Here the climate is sub-tropical and there are areas of wild beauty, like the mountains cracked by the heat, the rugged and rocky plateaus, the saltpans and marshes of Cabo de Gratas and the black beaches of Las Negras.

However, the climate has also encouraged tourism, especially on the coast at Roquetas del Mar and Aguadolce, and developed the agricultural economy based on greenhouse production on the plateau to the west of the Sierra de Gádor.

Oranges and wine grapes are produced in great quantities in the valley of Andarax whereas quarries and mines underpin the economy and dominate the landscape in the valley of Almazor.

One of the surprises of the geography of this province is the presence of many large caves dating back thousands of years; they are to be seen in the valleys of Andarax and Almazor, at La Chanca near the Arab fort in Almeria and close to Veléz Blanco and Veléz Rubio not far from the border with Murcia.

Of diametrically opposite interest is Mini Hollywood, an unexpected film-set a little north of the Sierra Alhamilla where "spaghetti westerns" and adventure films have been shot.

Almeria is one of the Andalusian provinces where landscapes have remained practically untouched by the inconsiderate hand of man; for example, the Sierra de los Filabres that almost cuts the province in half, is filled with natural treasures.

Having crossed the northern boundary into Granada, a magnificent view soon meets the eye: the dark bell-tower of Guadix set among the green hills stands out against the sky. And the small town not far from the city of Granada has another, more wonderful surprise in store: the underground caves dug out in ancient times are still inhabited by a small but significant number of "new men in the caves".

To the southwest, the plateau of Granada stretches flat and wide on this side of the hills of Malaga; to the north, the heights of the Betico System act as a natural border with the provinces of Jaén to the east and Cordoba to the west.

Jaén is the best Andalusian area for olive production; hundreds of rows of olive trees lend a green and silver sheen to the landscape and cover the undulations of the land, that rise towards the limits of the province, with an atmosphere of tranquillity.

Andalusia's largest river has its source in the province of Jaén in the Sierra de Segura that together with the equally famous Sierra de Cazorla is so mountainous that it is easy to forget that this is Andalusia. With the exceptions of Ubeda and Baeza, the only modestly large towns, the rest of the province is sprinkled with tiny and beautiful villages that seem to have shut their doors on the passing of time.

The magic of Segura de la Sierra, Cazorla and Cambil radiates from every white building in their natural and enchanting setting. Both wild and gentle, the land of Jaén has been a crossroads of great movements for centuries; in times of war like the reconquest and Civil War, and in times of peace, as much today as in Roman times.

The small town of Las Navas de Tolosa bears witness to the history of this "half-way land". A worthy rival in beauty, the province of Cordoba lies to the west where the Guadalquivir becomes a major river cutting through a fertile plain.

To the north of the Guadalquivir, the Sierra Morena is wedged between Extremadura and Castile. The low hills hide some of Spain's most important metal deposits and provide deer and boar with an ideal habitat. But the province of Cordoba is not only attractive for its natural environment. Man too has left his mark during his habitation along the Guadalquivir through the millennia; for example, at Almodóvar del Río where a spectacular Arab castle dominates the hills, at Medina Azahara, the excavated city of Abd-ar Rahman III, and also far from the river, at Priego de Córdoba, that boasts excellent Baroque architecture.

66 top The towers of the 14th-century Arab fort of Almodóvar del Río reach up to the sky. The white houses of the small town hug the hill from where the castle solemnly overlooks the right bank of the Guadalquivir.

66-67 Green, gray and silver hues dominate the countryside on the hills where olives are grown. Wine, olives and olive oil are the traditional natural products of Andalusia.

67 top left The white houses and minaret-shaped chimneys between the rocks are simply surface additions to the real houses of Barrio Troglodita of Guadix: the caves.

67 top right Cazorla is a quiet town built on the slopes of the mountain range of the same name. The presence of the crenellated castle lends further interest to the lovely setting.

68 top left When the English set foot in Andalusia in the early 1900s, they brought the game of golf with them. Today some of southern Europe's best golf courses lie around Huelva.

68 top right Palos de la Frontera lies just to the south of Huelva. It was once a fairly important port and today is mostly famous for having been Columbus's point of departure.

68-69 A short distance from the Guadalquivir, as it meanders north of Jerez, another large river winds its way towards the ocean. This is the Guadalete, which flows into the Atlantic at Cadiz.

69 top The Caleta is the name of the beach at Cadiz, a sandy crescent on the shore of the Atlantic.

69 bottom Mount Hacho gives a clear view of the Strait of Gibraltar and Ceuta, one of Spain's African enclaves.

The province of Seville lies to the southwest of Cordoba in an area that might be called the heart of Andalusia. Squeezed between the Sierra Morena and the wine-producing hills of Jerez, the Guadalquivir dominates the countryside. Once again it is along the course of the river that the colonizing peoples of Andalusia have marked their presence: the remains of Italica are nearby. Leaving behind the old Betis, one enters the province of Huelva. Andalusia's most western province is not a mixture of different landscapes like the others. A pleasant feature is the grooves in the soil created by the rivers with the most interesting effects to be seen in the nature reserve of the Coto Doñana. Following the coast as far as the city of Huelva, one finds another natural feature of great beauty: here the Río Tinto, so-called for the color imparted to the river by the reddish stones below, meets the Río Odiel. Their courses have created a marshy area known as the Marismas del Odiel where spoonbills and herons live. Close by are the golf courses created by the British for relaxation when they were not working in the mines. The name Huelva, however, does not only evoke images of mines but also the ancient mythical kingdom of Tartessos. What remains of the port of Palos de la Frontera, where Columbus left from on his voyage, represents a past age of daring enterprises of revolutionary importance. Not far from Palos the ground rises slightly and vines appear around Niebla and La Palma and to the south is the sanctuary of the Virgen del Rocío, the most popular place of pilgrimage in Andalusia. The province of Cadiz is just around the corner, with its beaches that pass Cabo de Trafalgar and end at Tarifa. Once more on the tracks of the Arabs, and with an ironic smile on the faces of those who do not know whether or not to believe in the geography established by man, a hop across the Strait of Gibraltar brings one to the Spanish beaches of Africa. Ceuta and Melilla are tiny parcels of land on the African continent that remained in the hands of the Spanish crown even after the end of the protectorate of Morocco in 1956. Morocco lies just outside the door but is pushing hard to enter, just as Spain has tried so many times to do with Gibraltar.

PASSAGE THROUGH ANDALUSIA

CORDOBA, THE CAPITAL OF CALIPHS

The Christian reconquest of present-day Andalusia began to achieve concrete results with the battle of Las Navas de Tolosa in 1211 after decades of failed attempts. Centuries had passed since the Arabs had taken possession of the region and Catholic Spain set about expanding its rule over one of Europe's richest areas. Under the Arabs, Andalusia had reached a very high level of development and civilization demonstrated not only by its literature, which has reached us thanks to the school of translators in Toledo, but also by its superb architecture seen right across the territory. What had previously been a favorite setting of the Romans became the land on which the unchallenged temples of Catholicism were raised after the banishment of the Arabs. The alternation of such differing and powerful civilizations turned Andalusia into an open-air museum.

To follow the route of the attacking Catholic forces, one has to start in the province of Jaén, the area through which all of Andalusia's conquering armies have passed. This is where Baeza and Ubeda are situated and from where the Christian forces first leashed their attacks on the Arabs. At Baeza, Baroque is the period most represented with the Palacio de Jabalquinto, the Plaza de los Leones and the Convento de San Francisco; in Ubeda there stands one of the most perfect examples of

Renaissance architecture – the chapel of El Salvador that overlooks the Plaza Vázquez de Molino. The church of Santa Maria Alcázar de Los Reales also faces onto this square and stands on the position previously occupied by a mosque. The balance, harmony and aestheticism of Islam's places of worship that were not destroyed by the fury of the avenging Christians offer the visitor a sense of what al-Andalus must have truly been like.

For example, the mosque in Cordoba is of marvelous beauty; Cordoba was the capital of the caliphate reconquered three years after Ubeda and Baeza in 1236. Construction of the *mezquita*, or mosque, that stands in the center of the city in the middle of a maze of alleyways, was begun in 785 under Abd ar-Rahman I and was terminated in 793. Then it was in the shape of a perfect square with an internal court in which eleven

70 top left The Capilla del Salvador in Plaza Vázquez de Molina in Ubeda is a masterpiece of pure Spanish Renaissance architecture.

70 bottom left The Palacio de Jabalquinto is the most attractive building in Baeza.

70 top right The dome of the church of Santa Victoria, patron saint of the city, can be seen among the white houses with biscuit-colored roofs.

70 bottom right The equestrian statue of the Gran Capitán stands over the Plaza de las Tendillas, the elegant heart of Cordoba.

71 A monument to Manolete, the popular toreador born in Cordoba in 1917, stands in front of the church of Santa Marina de Aguas Santas.

72 top left The bell-tower of the Mosque, which faces onto the north side of the immense complex, heralds one of Andalusia's most important buildings. San Rafael stands on the top of the tower and its 12 bells; the tower has been rebuilt on several occasions.

72 top right The countless doors that open in the walls of the mosque are each distinct in appearance. However, despite the fact that they can be dated to different periods, all of them feature meticulous decorations that embellish the arches and fill the spaces created by the overlapping of geometric designs with multicolored, often floral elements.

72-73 The size of the construction, originally rather smaller, can be gauged from the top of the Mosque's bell tower. In the foreground, palm and cypress trees can be seen growing among orange trees in the Patio de los Naranjos. More distant, the outline of the cathedral emerges from the naves of the mosque.

73 top The 14th-century Torre de la Calahorra was an Arab lookout over the Guadalquivir. The rooms inside the tower house the Municipal History Museum.

73 center The ancient stone bridge over the Guadalquivir was built in Cordoba by the Romans. Cordoba became a Roman colony in 169 BC.

73 bottom The picture shows the narrow interior of the Synagogue, which still preserves remains of fine plaster decorations. Cordoba Synagogue was built in 1314 and is the only one remaining in Andalusia. Worship of the Jewish religion was permitted until 1492 when Ferdinand and Isabella expelled the Jews from Spain.

spacious arches each opened onto a nave, but this was in fact just the first of four phases of construction and expansion that continued until the end of the 10th century. Under the patronage of Abd ar-Rahman II, nine more arches were added to the south side of the mosque between 833 and 848, then, within the space of 12 months, from 964 to 965, a new extension promoted by al-Haquem was added on the south side. Adornments and further expansions were completed, of which the most important was the *mihrab* (prayer niche) – the holiest place in the entire building. It was formed by three chapels and housed the *Koran*. The arches of the *mihrab*'s ceiling, covered with filigree arabesques, were the culmination of a series of sculptural and architectural works of art that included the polychrome columns, Byzantine ceiling mosaics and finely worked capitals. The building was still not finished however; a new burst of creativity was sponsored by Almanzor and saw the expansion of the eastern side with the construction of new arches and eight more naves. Further modifications during the dominion of the Arabs altered the mosque's overall appearance little. This glorious religious building, supposed to have been built on the ancient site of a Roman-Visigoth church dedicated by Reccaredo to St. Vincent, underwent further alterations with the arrival of the Christians. The place where Allah was

74 The interior of the Mosque is a maze of polychrome arches held up by slender marble columns that divide the huge spaces to create the naves. The huge increase in the number of columns was the result of massive expansion projects that had begun in 833.

75 top left The design of the intertwined and polylobate arches illuminated by light filtered from the skylights added during the second enlargement of the Mosque is of great fascination.

75 center left The original section of the Mosque is warmly lit from the Patio de los Naranjos.

75 bottom left Construction of the Cathedral began in 1523. The picture shows the building's superb ceiling.

75 top right Difficulty in internal illumination due to enlargements of the Mosque was resolved by the construction of domes fitted with

skylights. The Villaviciosa Chapel was later built below one of these domes, next to the Royal Chapel.

75 bottom right This marvelous 6'6"-tall shrine is kept in the Treasure Room at the extreme south of the complex. It was the work of Enrique de Arfe.

worshipped was modified to embrace the house of God. The current main entrance, the Door of Pardon, is a representative synthesis of this architectural transition; built in the 14th century, it merges Arab art with Gothic and Romanesque architecture. A tower that vaguely resembles the Giralda of Seville was built shortly after on the north side where the external altar to the Virgen de los Faroles stands – the Virgin of Lamps. Having already been reconsecrated as a church during the year of Cordoba's reconquest, the *mezquita* was later turned into a cathedral in 1523. Ferdinand and Isabella first, then Charles V later, ordered that the temple of the "infidels" should be gutted to make space for a Catholic place of worship. Many of the beautiful columns were destroyed and many other artistic decorations of inestimable value suffered the same fate. The process of "Catholicising" the mosque was continued up until 1766 with the closure of a series of naves, the construction of more than 52 chapels and the transformation of the *mihrab* into a sacristy.

Today the cathedral-cum-mosque is quite the strangest place of worship one can imagine: alongside the horseshoe arches decorated with verses of the *Koran* (Islam forbids the reproduction of the human figure) there are images of Jesus on the cross, adoring Madonnas and gaudy Baroque altars seen beside the forest of slender marble columns.

Perhaps more than faith, history has been the force behind this symbol of Cordoba. The city was already known and loved by the Romans when the famous bridge across the Guadalquivir and the first defensive walls were built, though the remains of that age can certainly not be compared to those built during Arab rule. Apart from the mosque, the Moors built monuments like the Torre de la Calahorra, the fortress near the river at the south end of the Roman bridge. The Tower is now the home of the city's history museum and has an interesting Carpet Room and another dedicated to the poet Góngora. More numerous are the buildings that date to the next period of which the Alcázar is the most famous. This was constructed on

76 top left and 77 top right Statues dedicated to important figures and events are found throughout the Arab-Andalusian-style gardens of the Alcázar. Three easily recognized sculptures show Christopher Columbus at an audience with the "reyes católicos".

76 top right and 77 top left The Alcázar of the Christian kings was built on land that had been previously occupied by the Caliph's palace. It takes its name from the Arab word al-qasr meaning palace-fortress. Massive towers, like the octagonal one at the main entrance and the square Lion Tower, form part of the thick walls.

76-77 and 77 bottom right The Alcázar of the Christian kings was built in 1328 by order of Alfonso XI. It was the setting for many episodes of historic importance: Columbus was received here by Isabella and Ferdinand before he set sail across the Atlantic; Boabdil, the last Moslem ruler of Granada, was detained here where the Catholic monarchs had stayed just before the decisive besiege of that city; later, the entire complex was used as a court by the Holy Inquisition. Today, centuries later, the exquisite gardens are an indication of the splendor that reigned here.

the orders of Alfonso XI in 1328 and later lived in by Ferdinand and Isabella during the siege of Granada. In this building, the Romanesque and Gothic decorations are mixed with elements of Arab art and the carefully kept gardens remind those of the Generalife in Granada. Churches built after the reconquest are no different and are characterized by a mix of styles to which details and finishings in Baroque fashion were added during the 17th and 18th centuries. Santa Marina, San Nicolás de la Villa, La Magdalena and San Lorenzo are all good examples of this category of church. However Cordoba was simply a city of mosques first and then a city of churches (there were about 3,000 mosques at the time of the caliphate) as there was also one of the very few synagogues to have survived in Spain and the only in Andalusia. This was erected in 1314 but only served as a place of worship until 1492 when the Jews were expelled but there still remain some lovely inscriptions of the *Psalms* on the arches, which were carved on the inside of a square building that was later transformed into a hospital and then a Catholic church. Evidence of the past presence of Jews in Cordoba is shown not only by the former synagogue on Jews' Road but also by the nearby Ghetto, their original quarter that stretches beyond Almodovar Gate.

The Ghetto is a maze of narrow, twisting alleys flanking Jews' Road, which leads into the Plaza de Maimónides dedicated to the famous Jewish

Cordoban philosopher. Here stands the city museum of bullfighting art. Not far away the Zoco, or area of crafts studios and workshops, can be found where leatherwork, pottery, woodwork and silver filigree has been practised for centuries. Cordoba is a trove of timeless artistic treasures including the paintings of Julio Romero de Torres, in the museum of the same name, and Goya and Zurbarán, held in the Provincial Museum of Fine Arts, as well as decorated courtyards and the Plaza de las Tendillas, the Cristo de los Faroles and the Plaza de el Potro. Cordoba has an incomparable beauty created by the great civilizations that it came in contact with during its succession of historical episodes.

78 top The ceiling of the cathedral of Jaén rests on a structure of enormous size, which combines Renaissance and Baroque elements. Fine plasterwork can be seen in the Chapel of St. Andrew.

78-79 This bird's eye view shows the majesty of the cathedral of Jaén. It took about 150 years to build it, starting in the 16th century on ground previously occupied by a mosque. In the background, the olive-covered land ripples away to the mountains.

MEDINA E JAÉN, ARTISTIC RIVALRY BETWEEN ARABS AND CHRISTIANS

79 top The remains of Medina Azahara, just a few miles from Cordoba, can only give a partial glimpse of the town's past grandeur. The Arab name means the "Shining City" and it was built by Abd-ar Rahman III in the 10th century to replace Cordoba as the capital of the caliphate.

79 bottom Construction of the citadel started in 936 on specially created terraces. A splendid palace and mosque were built at Medina Azahara and a network of channels distributed water, a fundamental element in Arab culture.

Situated close by this spectacular capital is the city that wanted to take its place, at least for certain functions, during the era of the caliphate. The city Medina Azahara was built by Abd ar-Rahman III in the 10th century and was expanded by his successors. The remains of the city are a pale semblance of the medieval city as they lie along the terraces built on the slopes of the Sierra mountains. The splendors of the unfortunate *medina* (city) were destroyed well before the reconquest when the Berbers were engaged in civil war with the Arabs throughout al-Andalus, at the beginning of the second millennium.

Returning to the path of the reconquest, nine years after Cordoba fell to the Christians, it was the turn of Jaén from which province the military operations against the Moslems had set out. The provincial capital seems to have a split personality where the splendidly restored Arab Baths are found alongside the superb Gothic/Baroque cathedral. The gems of the province are not all to be found in the city but also in the countryside like, apart from the towns of Baeza and Ubeda, the Santuario de Nuestra Señora de la Cabeza, the scene of strenuous resistance against the Republicans during the Civil War.

SEVILLE, SPLENDORS OF THE SIGLO DE ORO

*E*lsewhere, the architectural and artistic patrimony is even more interesting. Within a dozen years, the fate that befell Cordoba also befell Seville when Ferdinand III took possession of it in 1248. At the time, Seville was a splendid Moslem city boasting a range of magnificent buildings: the mosque, first and foremost, with its court of orange trees; the tower adjacent, the Alcázar, with its vaguely Granadine gardens, and the massive outpost looking over the Guadalquivir, the Torre del Oro. Like several other of Seville's Arab buildings, the mosque underwent transformation into the largest Christian church in Spain, the third biggest in the world after St. Peter's in Rome and St. Paul's in London. The only parts of the mosque to survive are the Patio de los Naranjos and the Giralda – the amazing tower built by Abu Yuqub Yusuf and his successor Almanzor Jacob. Seville cathedral was built in Gothic style within a hundred years starting from 1401. Later additions in late-Gothic style make the massive edifice (measuring 138 by 91 yards and 110 feet tall) even more interesting though it is not easy to get an idea of the building size without climbing the Giralda. Inside the cathedral, the enormous gilded wooden altar probably attracts the most attention. The Giralda is the symbol of Seville; it was partially destroyed in an earthquake in the 16th century but rebuilt with

80 top The Capillita del Carmen is a graceful chapel at the west end of the Guadalquivir bridge, which leads from the town center to Triana, the quarter once lived in by gypsies.

80 center The Casa de Pilatos is a splendid example of lay architecture from the 16th century. The main internal courtyard has a fountain with the bust of Janus in the center and is richly decorated in mudéjar *style with polychrome* azulejos *(enameled tiles). Two corners of the patio are occupied by statues of Pallas and Ceres whereas other mythological and historical subjects are found in every section of the house.*

80 bottom From the top of the Giralda, the tower that is considered the symbol of the city, the contradictory nature of Seville is clearly apparent: on the one hand, a city with a glorious past and a thousand beautiful monuments; on the other, it has its eye on the future that already appears to have arrived on the Isla de la Cartuja.

83 top left The vault between the choir-stalls and the Capilla Mayor along the central nave is a significant example of the spirit that guided construction of the cathedral. There are five naves in all to give overall dimensions of 377 feet long by 247 feet wide. The cathedral contains 50 other chapels besides this one.

84 and 84-85
The large Plaza de España is a surprising and well-lit semi-circle, which opens to the east into Maria Luisa Park. A canal follows the curve of the long portico and provides a setting for pleasure boats. The bridges over the water help to create a romantic atmosphere in this huge space overlooked by buildings housing the General Captaincy and the offices of the Civil Government and Military Government. One of the elements that gives most character to this architectural complex is the thousands of azulejos that cover the surfaces.

85 History and art mingle to give birth to the mosaics that adorn the Plaza de España. People, places and events from Andalusian and Spanish history are reproduced in the thousands of tiles, mostly colored in shades of blue.

Christians won back the city, the tower lost its primary function.

The history of Seville is told in its squares and streets through examples such as: the Barrio de Santa Cruz, with carefully maintained courtyards and clean lanes smelling of flowers and lemon and orange bushes, which used to be the Jewish quarter where the city finances were administrated; Triana which used to be a suburb inhabited by gypsies and now is an area famed for its nightlife; Plaza de España, which was inaugurated for the Ibero-American Exhibition of 1929 and has episodes of Spanish history painted on its *azulejos* (decorated ceramic tiles) and an unusual semi-circular design. But above all, the buildings are the keepers of the history of Seville when it was Queen of the Seas. The Lonja used to be the old goods exchange built on Isabella's orders and is now where most of the documents relating to Columbian and colonial America are stored. Alongside this not so nice building are others that are more attractive. The best known is the Casa de Pilatos with its multi-color tiled walls and a splendid courtyard where a statue of Minerva by the Greek sculptor Phidias stands.

The wonders in the museums of the Andalusian capital do not cease to amaze. Works of the Seville School of the 15th and 16th centuries can be seen in the Museum of Fine Arts with paintings by Zurbarán and Murrillo. The Hospital of Charity also boasts works by Murrillo. A large number of finds, including the famous treasure of El Carambolo, throw light on the past of ancient Hispalis (Seville) and all of Andalusia in the Archeological Museum. The welcoming and open city of Seville must have been an easy place to settle for the conquering civilizations, the Romans, the Arabs and the Catholic Spaniards.

Cadiz, on the other hand, was very different. It and the western region of al-Andalus were the next destinations of the reconquest forces and fell in 1263.

CADICE, THE WALLS OF RESISTANCE

86 top left The white houses of Cadiz stretch along the Atlantic coast just where the waters of the Guadalete flow into the sea. The thin strip of land on which the city stands ends with the Isla de León, a tiny peninsula cut by a canal.

86 top right and 87 The unmistakable outline of the New Cathedral of Cadiz dominates the old city center with its golden dome. Construction of the building began in 1720 with the adoption of a vaguely Baroque style but was terminated over a century later to undergo an increasingly classical influence.

86-87 At the start of the 20th century, a monument to the Cortes was erected in Plaza de España. It commemorates one of the most important events, not just in the history of Cadiz, but for the whole of Spain: the proclamation of the first constitution, which occurred in the city in 1812.

The etymology of the name Cadiz is based on the idea of a stronghold. It took the name Gadir, "fortified place", when it was founded by the Phoenicians around 1100 BC on an island just off the shore. For a long time it was the outpost of this people of navigators but they had to give way when the Romans arrived. The extraordinary position of this drop of land (which has been joined to the mainland for some centuries) made it a natural boundary between two worlds: between the reciprocally unknown Mediterranean and Atlantic in ancient times and between the Arab territory and reconquered Christian lands in the Middle Ages. The history of no other Andalusian city is more recounted by its geographical position than by its archeological remains. The walls that surround it date from the 17th and 18th centuries, 400-500 years after the reconquest had taken the area where the frontier had now been established. Alfonso X the Wise had taken Cadiz in 1263 and subsequently used the city as a base for operations against the Moors but it was only much later, when the city had prospered, that it was forced to defend itself, this time against the piratical incursions of the English. It took a long time though before the fortifications, the remains of which can still be seen today, were completed. The ancient city center opens inside the Puerto de Tierra. Despite Cadiz being the oldest still inhabited European city, its monuments are essentially Baroque or Neoclassical. The most interesting are the Old Cathedral, built at the start of the 17th century, and the church of St. Catalina. The New Cathedral, which dates from the 18th century and contains the remains of Luis de Falla and the Cárcel Real, the former royal prison, are more recent, built in Neoclassical style. Besides the military constructions and the tall, aristocratic, Neoclassical palazzi that line the streets of the center, there is a series of attractive squares like the Plaza de la Mina, overlooked by the city's historical museum, and the Plaza de España, where the Monument dedicated to the *Cortes* stands. The *Cortes* was the first true Spanish parliament; it met in 1812 when almost all the rest of the country was being put to the fire and the sword by Napoleon.

ARCOS, ALMERIA AND HUELVA, ANDALUSIAN FRONTIERS

There are other architectural jewels elsewhere in the province like the Arcos de la Frontera, a white town of ancient buildings, and Prado del Rey, a small city built by Charles III.

Just beyond the *Frontera* lies the present-day province of Huelva, which was taken back by the Christians at the same time as Cadiz. Two consequences of this event, still visible today, were the construction of the Franciscan hermitage at La Rábida, a place closely linked to Columbus's voyage to the New World, which was consecrated shortly after the arrival of

the Christians, and the magnificent bastions of Niebla, an ancient Arab town and capital of a kingdom that began to decline from that moment. Although the fortunes of Huelva expanded greatly compared to the Middle Ages, there are few traces of the peoples that lived there. Not only are there no remains of the Tartessians, but the passage of the Phoenicians, who founded it, Greeks, Carthaginians and Romans exists almost exclusively in the history books. More recently, the British semi-colonized this province and the area known as the Barrio Reina Victoria, the quarter built by the colonizers in the 1920s, bears witness to this fact.

Once the Catholic forces had got a firm foothold on the western territory of Andalusia, they were ready to make the decisive attacks and complete their conquest. Almeria, one of the richest *taifas* of the 11th century, had been under the influence of the Kingdom of Granada for some time, which was suffering from constant pressure on its northeastern border from the Spanish monarchy.

There are many ruins of castles dotted around the province of Almeria from its period of greatest glory under the Arabs. Foremost are the majestic walls of the Alcazaba, the Arab fortification that contains a court from a later period. Far from the old center where the modern section of the city stands, no trace is left of Almeria's past power.

88 left The massive castle of San Cristobal with the Chapel of the Templars is one of the main historical attractions in Andalusia's most eastern province, Almería.

88 right At 520 feet above the Guadalete, Arcos de la Frontera, in white, stands at the edge of the terrain. The religious buildings are Catholic and the palaces Arab. Arcos still retains signs of the long religious struggle.

88-89 The ruins of the walls of the Alcazaba, the Arab citadel built between the 8th and the 16th centuries, dominate the city of Almería that stands on the bay of the same name.

89 top left The unusual Barrio Reina Victoria is a district of Anglo-Saxon-style houses. They were built at the start of the 20th century when the English were present in the area.

89 top right The monument to Christopher Columbus erected in 1992 stands on Punta del Sebo in Huelva. Palos and the Monasterio de la Rábida are just a stone's throw away.

90 top left and 90-91 The remains of the old section of Malaga beyond the unfinished cathedral are mostly of Arab origin, like Gibralfaro castle from where there is an excellent panorama (90 top), and the ruins of the Alcazaba, surrounded by luxuriant vegetation that stretches right down to the front of the Town Hall (90-91).

MALAGA AND RONDA, TWO BRIDGES BETWEEN PAST AND FUTURE

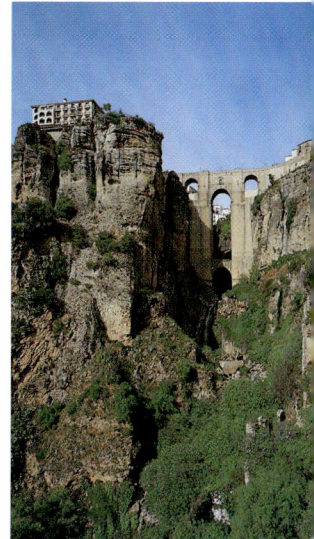

The first slice of Granada taken from the Arabs was the area around Ronda and Malaga. The birthplace of bull-fighting, Ronda is magnificently situated on the hills north of Malaga. The Arab township was connected to the new city (dating from the 16th century) by the spectacular Puente Nuevo. This triple-arched bridge was begun in 1755 by the architect José Martín de Aldehuela. It is more than 75 yards long and spans the Tajo gorge, 550 feet deep, over the river Guadalevin. Ronda has a series of buildings that are surprising for their historical and artistic value. With the exception of the Church of the Espiritu Santo, built in 1485 when the city was retaken and which is only worthy of attention from a historical viewpoint, the most interesting building is the church of Santa Maria la Mayor. This blends a number of styles, late Gothic, Baroque and Renaissance, in the construction based around its tower that used to be an ancient minaret. The Arab influence is easily distinguishable at Ronda; there are the remains of the city walls, the Arab Baths, the Casa del Gigante with its lovely 14th-century decorations – and the Arab bridge has been completely rebuilt. *Mudéjar* art, the style that was current after the Spanish conquest of Andalusia and heavily influenced by Arab art, can be seen in an Arab patio in the Palacio de Mondragón though the building has a Renaissance façade. Although of different styles, also interesting are the Palacio del Marqués de Salvatierra, and the Casa del Rey Moro, a 19th-century construction with gardens and spectacular stairways.

When the Catholics readied themselves to take Granada's port, Malaga, they could count among the regained territories one of al-Andalus's greatest pearls, Ronda, which they greatly embellished. After nearly 700 years of Islamic rule, Malaga, the outlet to the sea of the Kingdom of Granada, was besieged by the Catholics and forced to surrender in 1487. Although the origins of Andalusia's second city date back to the Phoenicians, it has no important buildings or monuments from before the Arab era. The Alcazaba and Gibralfaro Castle are the most important, and then there are the unfinished 16th-century cathedral and the late-Gothic Church of the Sagrario, built on the remains of a mosque.

90 top right The classic image of modern Malaga is of tall buildings along the shore and the bull-fighting arena. Malaga is an important

contributor to the Andalusian economy with traditional agriculture in its hills and tourism in continuous expansion on the coast.

91 top The Puente Nuevo in Ronda is suspended nearly 500 feet above the Tajo gorge.
It was built in the middle of the 18th century to connect the old part of the town with the new part.

91 bottom As well as its famous bridge, Ronda has buildings of great architectural interest. One of these is the Casa del Rey Moro surrounded by a lovely garden in the center of the Arab section of the town.

GRANADA, AT THE FEET OF THE RED FORTRESS

Without its port, Granada's time seemed to be running out, but it was still some years before Boabdil was forced to leave for exile and Ferdinand and Isabella victoriously entered the city. The Christian reconquest of Andalusia was ended in 1492, the same year in which Columbus set off from Palos and more than 200 years since the famous battle of Sierra Morena. Granada, heart of the Moslem resistance, fell to the *"reyes católicos"* after a drawn-out siege and the gates of the most spectacular medieval Arab citadel in all of Spain were opened to the Christians. This was of course the Alhambra or "red castle" built by Yusuf I and his son Mohamed V between 1333 and 1391. The palace that Charles V had built inside the Alhambra in 1526 contrasted strongly with the original architecture but did not diminish its beauty. Located in a superb position within the city, the Alhambra is rendered even more splendid by the magnificent views it commands from its every corner over the plain, Sacromonte and the Albaicín, the Arab quarter of small white houses. Aljibes square and the Tower of the Vela, for example, are two extraordinary vantage points but every section of the Alhambra is breathtaking. There is the Generalife, the summer residence of the Moslem court, where a thousand species of rose grow amidst the beautiful fountains. Of the three palaces that make

92 *The fascination of Granada is mostly found as one wanders through the alleyways next to the Albaicín, the Arab district. Lovely old houses line the river Darro that separates the hill of the Alhambra from the hill of the Albaicín.*

92-93 *The hill of Sacromonte is topped by the abbey of the same name from where there is a fine view of the Alhambra. Historically, Sacromonte was the* district *lived in by gypsies but today it is losing these inhabitants. Occasionally, however, the notes of a* flamenco *can be heard from within the white houses.*

93 top The view of Granada from the walls of the Alhambra is simply spectacular. The elegant buildings, churches and bell-towers in the center of the city are set against the backdrop of palms, cypresses and other trees that line the streets and squares.

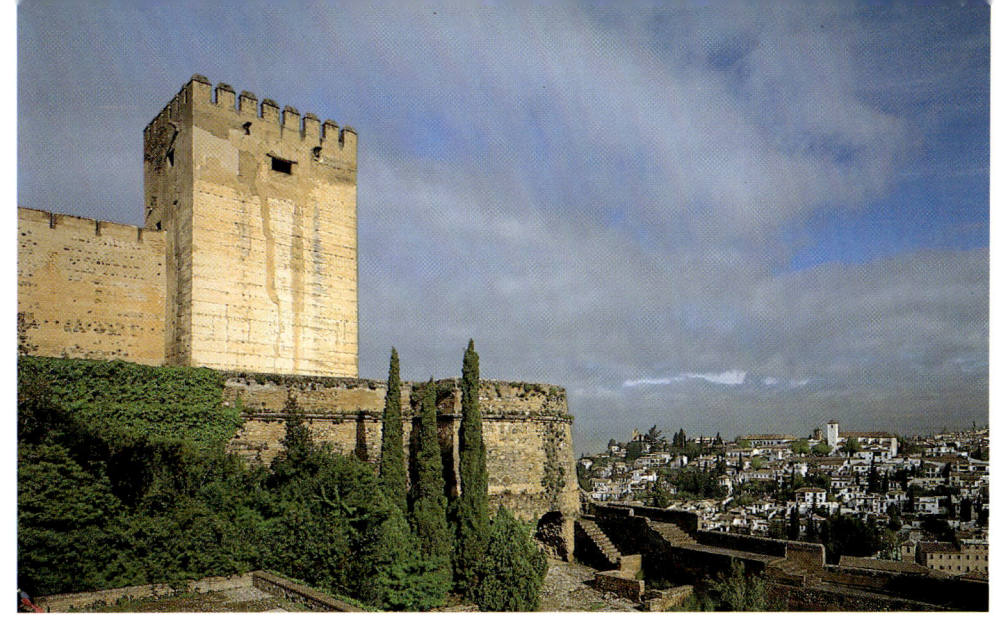

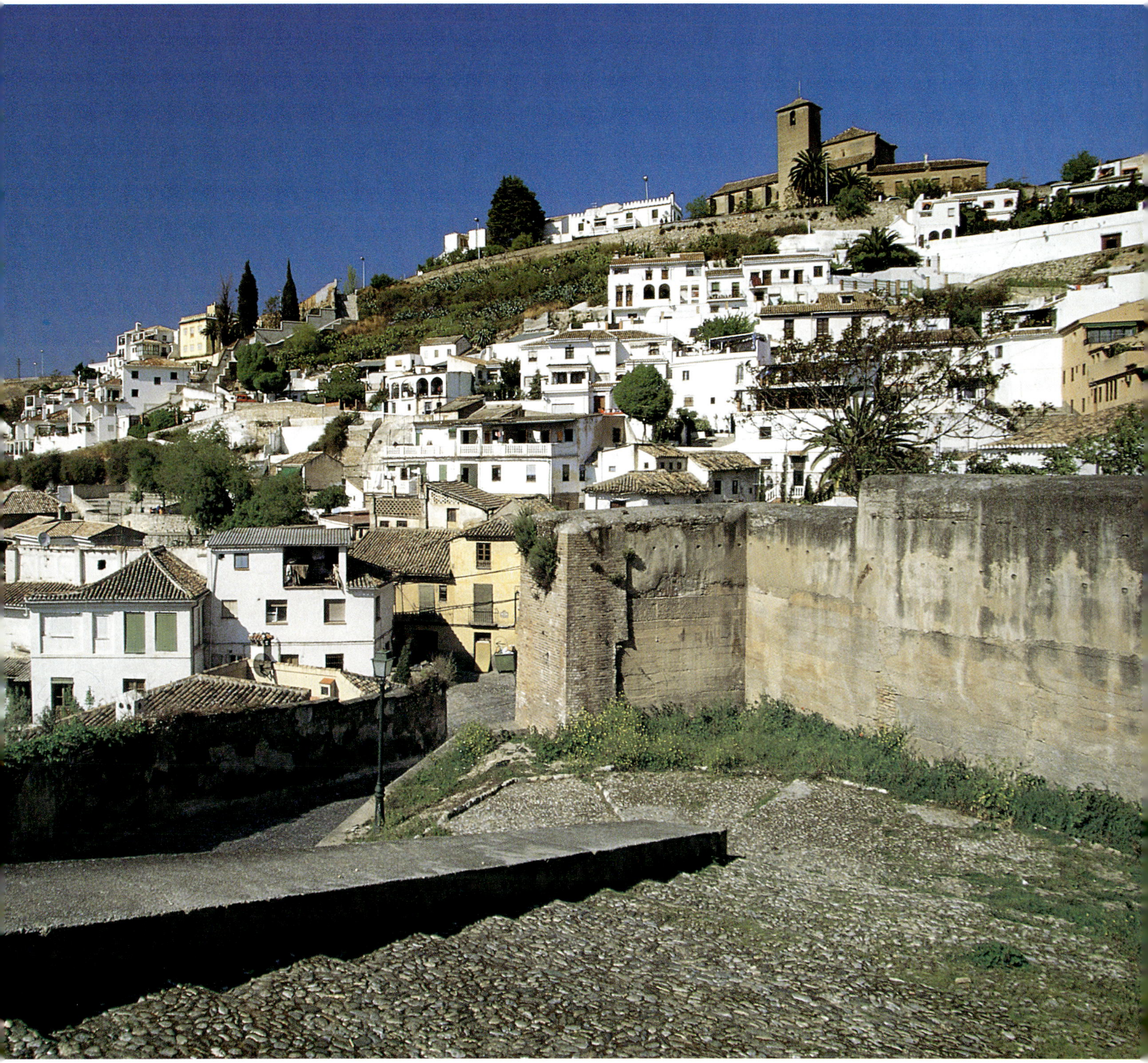

up the old royal apartments – Mexuar, Serrai and Harem – the Serrai is the most spectacular with its ceramic decorations, stuccoes and inlaid ornamentation of infinitely-repeated motifs and verses taken from the *Koran* or poetry. The famous courtyards are simple, like the Patio de los Arrayanes, or filled with slender columns, like the Patio de los Leones. Especially wonderful are the Ambassadors' Room with its exquisite ceiling decorations, the Royal Baths decorated with colored *azulejos*, and the palace of Charles V, the most beautiful Renaissance building outside of Italy.

When the Catholics took Granada, they did not simply transform the Alhambra but followed the example they had practised elsewhere of replacing or modifying the Arab buildings that adorned the city.

The mosque was replaced with a cathedral and a Royal Chapel built next door; the chapel acts as the tomb of Ferdinand and Isabella and also has a collection of 16th-century Dutch paintings. Some Arab buildings still remain, other than the Alhambra, in memory of the "infidels" such as the 11th-century Bañuelo, the Arab Baths and the 15th-century palace of Dar al-Horra.

Architectural masterpieces from after the conquest are the San Juan de Dios Hospital, with frescoed and tiled *patios*; the Royal Hospital,

96 top The Monastery of Cartuja (Charterhouse) was built high up in the north of the city of Granada, far from the center but close to the Albaicín.

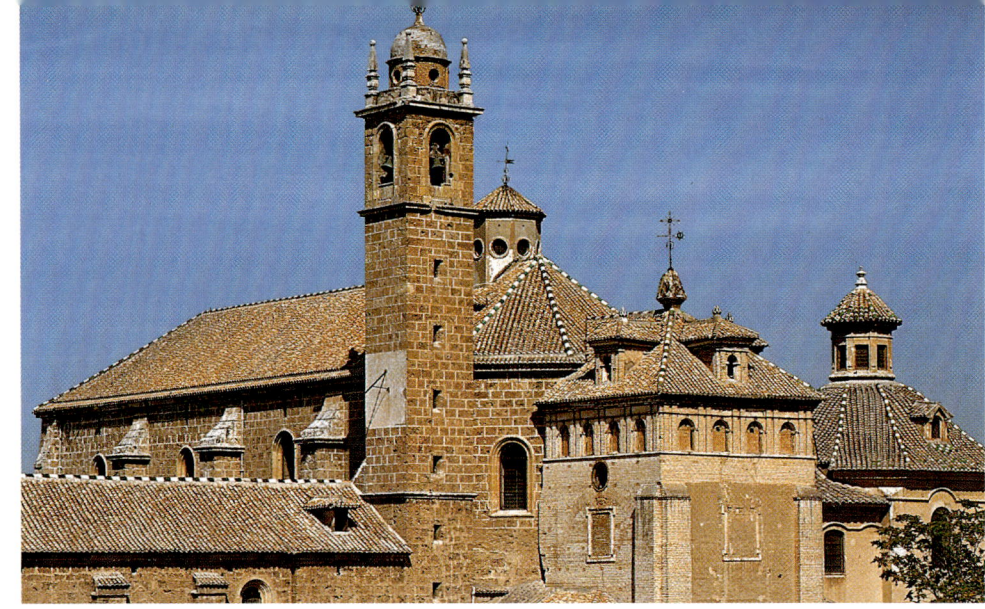

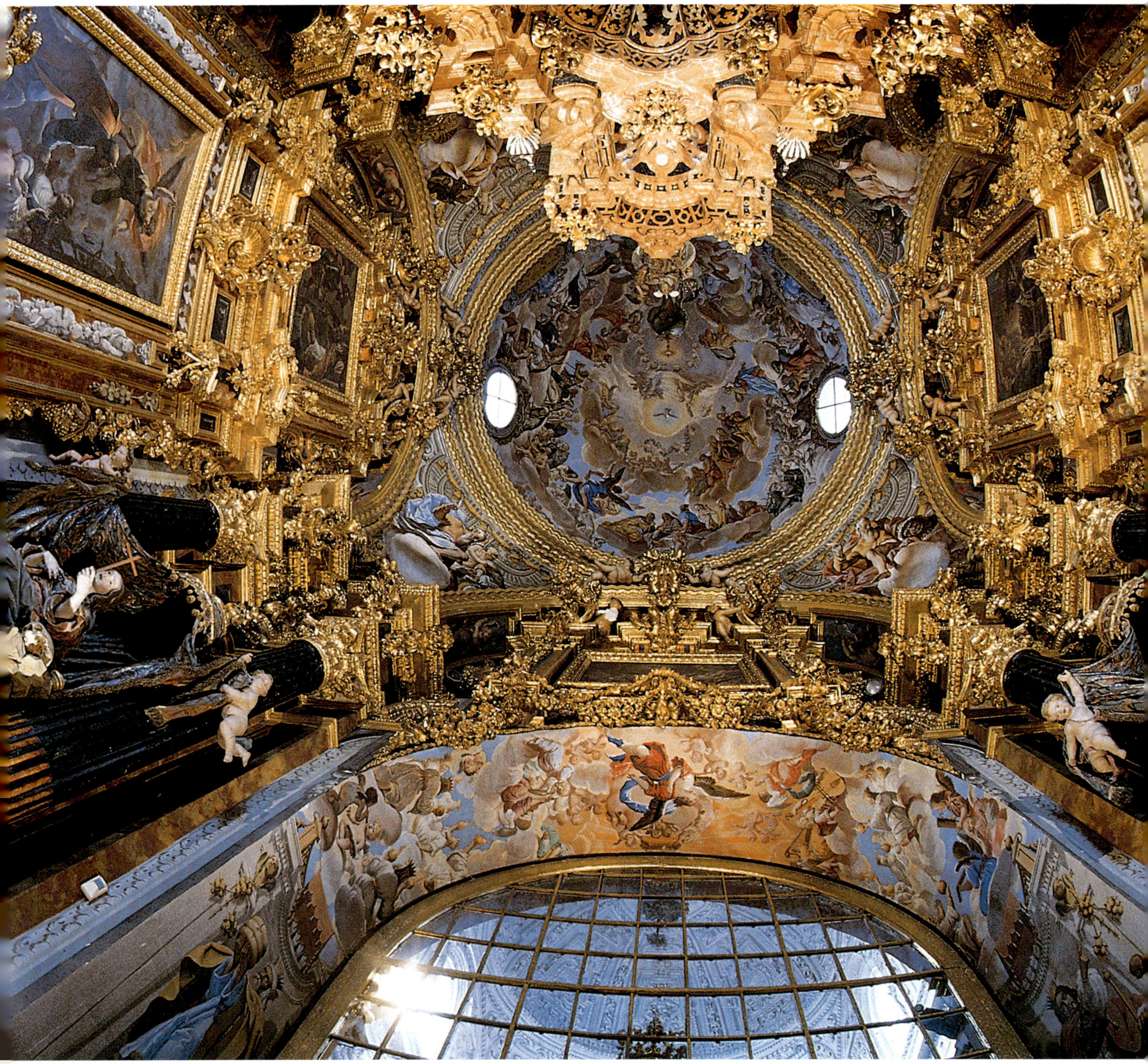

now the home of the university's administrative offices; the university itself, founded by Charles V in 1526, today one of the largest in the country and also occupying several other buildings scattered around the city. The Faculty of the Arts stands near the Monasterio de la Cartuja, a splendid example of Spanish Baroque architecture that overlooks the city from the top of a hill. Near the old buildings, there are areas of peace and harmony, like the Plaza Bibrambla, or places from the past, like the Albaicín, reminders of when the Andalusia was Arab.

96-97 *In contrast to its exterior design, the interior of the Cartuja is an extravaganza of Baroque architecture. This is the ceiling of the Sancta Sanctorum.*

97 left *The Cartuja was built and decorated between the 16th and 17th centuries. It is certainly one of the most important examples of Churraresque Baroque architecture in all of Andalusia. The spiral columns, the gilded stuccoes, the statues of angels and the bright, densely colored frescoes are characteristic of the Sancta Sanctorum.*

97 right *The Hospital of San Juan de Dios was founded by St. John of God in 1536 and is one of the most interesting buildings in Granada. It is designed around two patios and is decorated with frescoes showing the life of the founder-saint. Its splendid 18th-century basilica is considered a Baroque masterpiece.*

98 This view from
above shows what
remains of the
Alcazaba, the fort
built inside the
Alhambra to defend
the royal Palace.

99-102 The buildings
inside the Alhambra
are seen to best
advantage from the
gardens of the
Generalife. On the
left stands the
imposing palace of
Charles V; the
crenellated towers on
the right are part of
the Alcazaba
fortifications.

103 top The lower section of the western façade of Charles V's palace retains the only original elements still to be seen. Four pairs of Doric columns support a cornice decorated with a frieze featuring triglyphs and metopes.

103 bottom The palace of Charles V was built during the first half of the 16th century and is considered the most important Renaissance-style building outside of Italy. Inside, there is a wide circular court surrounded by a classical colonnade.

104 top left The internal face of the palace where the ruler carried out his diplomatic duties, the Serrai, is reflected in the pool in the center of the Patio de los Arrayanes.

104 top right The Patio de los Arrayanes is also known as the Patio de los Mirtos because of the hedgerows of myrtle that run along its two longer sides. The Patio de los Arrayanes is an example of typical courtyard-cum-garden.

104-105 The Patio de los Leones is without doubt the symbol of the entire Alhambra. It was built in the 14th century during the reign of Mohammed V and takes its name from the lions that hold up the tank in the center of the court.

105 The Patio de los Leones has undergone repeated renovation work. The central fountain today appears in its original form but was for a long time topped by another, smaller fountain, which is now placed in the garden of the Adarves.

106 top Paintings on leather line the lovely barrel vault in the Kings' Room, also known as the Hall of Justice. The picture on the ceiling of the central alcove shows the 10 kings of the Nasrid dynasty conferring.

106 center Perhaps the most sober of the Arab palaces in the royal residence, the Mexuar is the only section open to the public. It was here that justice was administered and bureaucratic procedures were carried out. From the 18th century up until a few years ago, the largest room in the Mexuar was fitted out as a chapel.

106 bottom With its finely decorated loggias, the Mirador de Lindaraja is a true masterpiece of Moslem art. It faces a garden created in the 16th century as decoration for the newly built Emperor's Rooms.

106-107 The Sala de las dos Hermanas (the Room of the two Sisters) is topped by an octagon based dome decorated with marvelously refined plasterwork.

108 *An irrigation channel with small water spouts inside the Patio de la Acequia accompanies the gaze towards one of the buildings of the Generalife. The extent of the irrigation system in the tropical gardens permits the Generalife such varied and thick vegetation.*

109 top left *A fountain ordered by the Christians after the reconquest stands in the center of the Lindaraja gardens, but the tank it stands on is still Arab in shape. This mixture of styles is typical of the Alhambra as a whole.*

109 bottom left and top right *Built to accommodate the Arab rulers during the hot season, the Generalife is above all appreciated for the beauty of its gardens. The long avenues decorated with flowers that connect the gardens are the settings for explosions of color and clouds of floral scents.*

109 bottom right *Fountains add to the attractiveness of the courtyards in the gardens of the Generalife.*

Festivals and celebrations in Andalusia are not just Hemingwayesque folklore for the benefit of tourists but a perpetuation of ancient rituals that have their roots in the past more or less remote. There are more than 3000 festivals celebrated during the year across 800 districts in Andalusia. That means that every day almost 10 celebrations on average take place throughout this enchanting province. Too often emphasis is put on the diversionary aspect of Andalusian festivals without considering that any weekend spent in Andalusia would provide entertainment; even worse, the historical element is often ignored. Such flippancy could lead to a superficial interpretation of these public displays that for hundreds of years have delighted generation after generation of Andalusians who treat them with devotion, enthusiasm and seriousness.

Famous, fascinating and ostentatious, the Holy Week celebrations in Seville are without doubt the mirror of Andalusian history. The first processions date back to 1248 when the city was liberated from Arab domination by Ferdinand III of Castile. The Catholic triumph was celebrated with jubilation but, in the centuries that have followed, the festival has experienced varying degrees of success depending on historical events. In the 15th century when there were still no rules that governed it, the processions were limited to the Wednesday, Thursday and Good Friday of Holy Week. The confraternities that exhibited their statues often created disruption in the city streets. In 1510, the route was made to begin at the house of the Marquis of Tarifa, Casa Pilatos, "Pilate's House", a tag it still maintains. The end of the route was decided to be Cruz del Campo, outside the city, which could be reached by walking 3,333 *pasos*, or paces, just as Jesus did on the day of the Crucifixion. Between the 14 stations, 472 Pater Nosters were recited. This was the period of greatest splendor in the Holy Week processions in Seville. The Council of Trent in 1545 also affected this aspect of Catholic religious life. Seville was experiencing a moment of glory thanks to commercial success overseas and its trade in precious materials brought it increasing wealth.

The *Siglo de Oro* saw the highest manifestation of culture throughout the entire Iberian peninsula; any episode of everyday life could be transformed into art while the extraordinary wealth of the Church and the availability of its funds made it possible for simple statues to be turned into works of art. The *imagineros*, craftsmen who produced wooden statues imbued with a life of their own, gave the figures of Mary and Jesus human expressions. Crying, suffering faces able to

110 top left A paso with the Virgin Mary pushes its way through the crowds in the streets of Seville. The paso *is the combination of the support and the holy image and may be of Christ, the Virgin Mary or a representation of Christ's Passion.*

110 bottom left Each hermandad (confraternity) accompanies its own paso and wears a distinguishing habit. The brothers have their faces covered but may or may not fasten the conical hat, depending on whether they are nazarenos or simple penitentes.

110 top right and 111 top right Nazarenos are members of the confraternity that parade wearing the capirote (conical hat) as they carry candles or insignia in the procession. Members of the confraternity keep their faces covered to maintain their anonymity.

111 left The statue of the Santissimo Cristo de la Sed crucifix is held up by a Baroque-style support decorated with hundreds of carnations and other flowers. Most of the statues are true works of art in the old tradition of the imagineros, *the craftsmen that made holy images.*

111 bottom right Women who take part in the Holy Week processions wear a short black dress and the traditional mantilla, *the piece of lace that hangs down from the comb on top of the head.*

112 The picture shows the cloak of the Virgin of the Real Cofradía de Nuestra Señora de los Dolores of Granada, a province in Andalusia where the Easter parades have a great following. The pasos of the Virgin Mary are without doubt the most spectacular. The statue of Mary is covered with a beautifully embroidered cloak.

113 left Holy Week in Granada is a very heartfelt affair. The streets are filled with crowds that follow the pasos or watch the procession from a vantage point. The confraternities are dressed in their habitual robes and march proudly beside their statues.

113 top right The route from Sacromonte to Plaza Nueva along the river Darro in Granada is very lovely. The corteges squeeze into the narrow lane behind the Albaicín before filling the square with color.

113 center right The costaleros (bearers of the statues) parade with their loads. Men used to be hired to carry the pasos but now the brothers perform the task themselves.

113 bottom right The paso of Jesus Entering Jerusalem opens Granada's Easter processions.

arouse deep emotion in the faithful that accompanied the passage of the richly dressed figures on the Easter parades became the symbol of the power of Seville under the mask of religious fervor. Although in 1605 the church of Seville found itself forced to impose rules so that the ceremony might be performed more smoothly. As the confraternities and the statues they carried were increasing dramatically in number, so routes, stops, schedules and sequences were established. And it was during this period that the Baroque wooden figures carried in the procession took the name of *paso*.

The advent of the Age of Enlightenment brought with it the exaltation of reason and a more radical scepticism with the result that Holy Week in Seville began to wane. At the same time, the progressive decline of this Andalusian port placed a heavy restriction on the pomp of previous decades, diminishing its glory and spectacle. The failing economy was only the prelude to a serious crisis that progressed with the approach of the Napoleonic threat.

The first years of the 19th century brought death and destruction to Andalusia and these adverse conditions made it increasingly difficult to keep up this tradition. It was only in 1834, with the restitution of assets that had been confiscated from the Church of Seville, that the city's most troublesome festival began

once more to see its former glory. But Seville was obliged one more time to put a brake on the enthusiasm and bow to the force of history: the Civil War at the beginning of the 20th century brought new losses when all the holy statues that could not be hidden were either lost, damaged or destroyed.

Today, after so many hardships, Seville's Holy Week has achieved a level of popularity, participation and enthusiasm to render it unique in the world. More than 100 *pasos* are paraded through the streets for an entire week, escorted by the brothers. The slow, regular pace of the passing images is accompanied by a praying crowd. Every so often, the statues stop and a *saeta* – a nostalgic gypsy oration in song – is heard from a balcony or window and the crowd falls silent. Then, the *capataz*, a sort of orchestrator of maneuvers, bangs a clapper fixed to the pedestal of the statue to signal it should be raised. The *costaleros*, the *paso* bearers that number between 36 and 48, lift it in one go, the crowd applauds, a thrill runs through even the most secular of laymen and the statue slowly restarts its journey.

In Granada, thanks to scenaries of great fascination such as the Alhambra or the Albaicín, Easter processions, which are very popular, are particularly charming.

Different in spirit but equally linked to historical events, or rather, char-

114 top The roots of the Seville Fair go back to medieval traditions. Today the fair is Seville's most famous secular event. Carts and horses are rigged out and paraded through the streets of the city and the fair district led by people wearing traditional Andalusian costume.

114-115 Any moment of the day is good to take the horses through the streets of the fair. Since the early 1970s, the fair has been held in the Prado de San Sebastián where a temporary city is created able to welcome thousands of revellers from 18 April each year.

115 The horsemen who are a central feature of the fair must all wear the same special clothing, regardless of age or sex. The trousers that accompany the short jacket may be grey or black, the shirt must be white. The wide-rimmed and rigid sombrero is encircled by a band of satin or velvet. The uniformity of dress is not a limitation of personal expression but more a question of demeanor.

acters from history, another festival takes place in Seville shortly after Easter. This is the Feria de Abril (April Fair). It is a truly secular affair that has its roots in the agricultural fairs of the 13th century. In 1292, Alfonso X the Wise, the famous Spanish monarch remembered more for his cultural than military undertakings, issued the Charter of Concession that officially granted Seville the right to hold two fairs, one of which has succeeded in reaching the third millennium. In fact, the modern emphasis of the fair held on 18 April dates from 1847 when Isabella II signed the ancient charter. Since then it has developed into the worldliest of the region's events. Thousands of people come from all over Spain and abroad to take part in the entertainments and dancing.

The center of activities was the Prado de San Sebastián until 1973 but is now the Campo de la Feria, which gets filled to overflowing with small, wooden houses covered with brightly colored canvases. Every self-respecting family or social group has one and invites guests to dance, drink wine and eat from dusk till dawn. Music is the most important element of this fair, which pulls a huge gaily dressed crowd to an *ad hoc* wooden city.

The Sevillanas (Seville dances) fill the air with irresistible rhythms while colored skirts swirl at every *vuelta* (turn) and twitch in the *pisoteo* (steps danced to rhythms marked by the stamping of heels on the ground). When the sun begins to rise after a night of high spirits, the dances end and silence returns to the makeshift village until the next evening. In the city, the fair has a point of reference in the Plaza de la Real Maestranza, the Baroque-style arena that faces onto the Guadalquivir.

116-117 Gorgeous in their colored costumes, Andalusian women twirl between the tented houses of the fair. Institutions and associations of all kinds outfit these temporary shelters made of frames and a colored covering; inside there are different types of food and drinks to be tasted and the dancing lasts all day long. The music is mostly made up of Sevillanas that often sing the praises of the fair itself; they can be heard everywhere, inviting the people to dance. Inside and outside the shelters, the clapping of hands sparks high spirits; there is no need to wait – someone is already twirling and stamping their feet.

118 and 119 top Equally for men and women, the traje *(clothing worn during the fair) is also an expression of identity. Awkward, delicate, sometimes uncomfortable and often fairly expensive, the clothes, especially for the women, may have a thousand variations all equally festive and highly colorful. A matching necklace and earrings nearly always frame the faces of the Sevillan women who, with hair drawn up and adorned with flowers or ribbons, prepare to revel in the exuberance of the fair.*

118-119 The entrance to the fair is a massive structure that is lit up as darkness falls. The tents are also lit up and prepare to welcome the thousands of people who spend the long night singing and dancing sustained by glasses of good wine.

120 left The horses trained at the Real Escuela Andaluza de Arte Ecuestre in Jerez are exhibited during the Feria del Caballo (Horse Fair) that takes place in the city in May. The school also trains jockeys.

120-121 and 121 top right The bull-fighting season is in full swing at the time of the Seville fair. Bull-fighting, of which the Sevillan public is a critical judge, is a sort of mystical celebration, a symbolic ritual.

120 right and 121 top left The bull-ring in Ronda was the cradle of bull-fighting. Built in 1785, it is thought to be the loveliest in the country. Each year in September, this arena is the setting for bull-fights in traditional costume.

At this time of the year, the Seville bull-fighting season is in full swing. It runs from Easter until the end of May. The importance of the fights is beyond dispute and anything but unknown. The *corrida* is practically a religious, mystical rite and is the central event of the festival day. The spectacle has a different atmosphere depending on where it takes place: the public in Seville seems more refined and demanding. They are silent and empathetic but occasionally ruthless in their judgement of *torear*, the art of bull-fighting. Although the arena in Seville is perhaps the most highly praised in Andalusia, the art of bull-fighting was created in Ronda in the 17th century with the famous *toreador* Romero. Even now, the Plaza de Toros in Ronda is the most important historically. Lying in green hills, it has seen many of the most famous *toreadors* in the history of bull-fighting. For more than two centuries, the *Rondeña* bull-fighting school has outshone all its rivals and its *corridas,* with the *toreadors* dressed as they were at the time of Goya, are major events.

The bulls are not the only animals in Andalusian festivals; horses are always a feature. If not historical in the strict sense of the word, horses have at least been a part of Andalusia's history. The fiery steeds that are now the pride of Jerez were animals of the desert brought by the Arabs when they invaded in 711 that quickly supplanted the local breed. The decline of al-Andalus did not put an end to the close relationship between the Arab breed and Spain. In 1019, Jerez obtained the royal privilege enabling it to hold a horse fair once a year. Since then, during the first half of May, splendid stallions have paraded through the streets of the city mounted by expert riders, often from the Royal Andalusian School of Equestrian Art. Breathtaking exhibitions delight the crowds that arrive from all over Spain.

There is no shortage either of music and dancing though the excesses of Seville are not to be found here. Dancing the *Sevillana*, the *Fandanguillo* or the *Flamenco* is not simply an academic exhibition but nor is it just another way to enjoy oneself. Besides demonstrating the skill necessary to move the body and feet in time following set steps with any of a thousand variations, the dancer is expressing a profound sense of life. Andalusian dances have their roots in the gypsy lament transformed into melody and it is thanks to the fusion of gypsy and Andalusian cultures that the most original music, songs and dances in all Spain have taken shape.

A guitar, castanets and a melancholy or joyful voice make the *bailaor* (dancers but only of these dances) spin like butterflies on flowers while the rhythmic clapping warms the atmosphere in a crescendo of enthusiasm. Andalusians are unique in this aspect of folklore – the expressiveness they demonstrate during a dance is total and unequivocal. Although many theories regarding supposed "Andalusianness" are debatable, there is no evidence that the one that postulates dance interpretation can be refuted. Once again, a series of historical events, beginning in the 15th century with the arrival of the gypsies into Spain, has contributed to a characteristic of the Andalusian people that shows itself in times of celebration.

122 left Dancing and singing to the sound of the guitar are two ways of self-expression that the Andalusian soul has transformed into art. The Flamenco *is the most famous dance, perhaps also the most mysterious and therefore fascinating. The origin of the* Flamenco *goes back to the arrival of the gypsies in Andalusia. The mixture of oriental and indigenous sounds gave birth to one of the West's most distinctive musical traditions.*

122 right Variations of the Flamenco *dance movements are infinite and intense technical preparation is required to be able to perform, even if only for fun.* Flamenco *schools have sprung up all over Andalusia to teach students from an early age.*

123 *The clothes and shoes worn during performance of the Flamenco are of great importance and not only for choreographic reasons. The skirt is made to twirl in accompaniment to the movement of the whole body while the heels of the shoes are stamped on the floor with energy and precision to a cutting rhythm. The movements of the hands are also an art within an art; the neatness of the designs created in the air and the positions of the fingers that accompany each note are the result of study and continuous, passionate practice.*

124 top Shortly after the end of Holy Week, the inhabitants of Granada start preparing for the next festival, El Día de las Cruces (the Day of the Crosses). Despite appearances, it is one of the most pagan festivals imaginable and an occasion to meet people, eat well, have a drink and dance.

One of the most important occasions is without doubt the Fiesta de las Cruces, the Day of the Cross. Granada is the heart of this popular festival that takes place in the first week of May. The symbolic element of the celebration is the "pagan" cross erected in each district of the city, in every square, in every place of importance, at the university and even in discotheques. The crosses are decorated with flowers (particularly carnations), fruit, vegetables and ceramics painted blue and green. They are almost treated as if they were to be judged for beauty. Beneath each cross there is a counter that distributes *tapas* (snacks) and rivers of wine to anyone who asks. People dance all around the cross; many are women in frilly Andalusian dress with shawls, *peinete* and *tacones* (hair slides and high-heeled dancing shoes) but many are also dressed simply for a party. Jeans and T-shirts are often to be seen swirling among the costumes but just as skillfully because the art of enjoying oneself is always and everywhere something that comes from within. While the *Sevillanas* mark the rhythm of the night down in the city, up in Sacromonte, in the rock-dwellings that are still inhabited, the gypsies perform the miracle of the *Flamenco*. As in every other Andalusian celebration, the sacred and the profane play an equal part, but the origin of this celebration is purely pagan – a toast to spring.

124-125 Large crosses decorated with freshly cut flowers, fruit and copper and ceramic containers are set up in every corner of the city. The festival lasts for a weekend, generally at the beginning of May, during which time food, drinks and music are available to every passer-by wherever there stands a cross.

125 During the festival, courtyards, meeting places and even bars compete to make their cross the most beautiful. The higher, brighter and more richly decorated it is, the more passers-by stop to admire it and toast the spring.

It is always the people that are the protagonists in any celebration in Andalusia. The people organize, prepare, participate, remember and plan for the year to come. They make themselves available almost unconditionally so that everything comes together to maximum effect as happens at Cordoba in the Fiesta de los Patios. In the ancient capital of the caliphate at the start of May, the residents open the doors of their houses and let every passer-by look into the most intimate section of the building, the *patio*. The *patio* originated with the Arabs and is a possible relative of the peristyle of the classical world. It is a world of its own revealing its magnificence in the name of an ancient tradition. The Andalusian *patio* is four-sided, surrounded by columns often covered by climbing plants and is a harmonious and silent universe free of any element suggestive of confusion. Plants, flowers, fountains, pots and ceramic tiles all help to create a mystical balance of relaxation and beauty. The summer heat fades away under the light that filters from above and the *patio* becomes an ideal place for a tryst, a prayer or a moment of meditation. In contrast to the uproar of the traditional festivals, the Fiesta de los Patios is an invitation to enter the atmosphere of *A Thousand and One Nights* when women told stories while men listened. The festival too is in a certain sense a legacy of the history; the nomadic Arabs settled in Andalusia and created the atmospheres they loved.

126 top and 126-127 The white walls of Cordoba that enclose each house's patio, oases of coolness and peace away from the bustle of the city, are literally overgrown with plants and flowers. Closely related to both Arab and Roman courtyards, the patio is a combination of art and nature used for meetings, solitary thoughts or learned conversation. Dozens of terracotta pots brimming with geraniums and ferns compete with climbing plants to beautify the walls and create a space of rare charm.

127 In May, Cordoba opens its patios and a competition is held to judge the most beautiful. Sometimes a graceful fountain in the shade is the distinctive element or a profusion of red geraniums hanging from whitewashed walls. Each year a burst of creativity and taste combines the colors, forms and scents of tropical plants, ivy and citrus trees.

128 Large groups arrive from all over Spain having traveled entire days with few outdoor stops.

Every year at Pentecost, pilgrims head for the tiny village of Ayamonte to pay homage to the Virgin.

129 The hooves of the oxen and horses pulling the carts on pilgrimage clop down the dusty road alongside those on foot.

The trip is long and tiring but it is the price to be paid to worship the Blanca Paloma, the Virgen del Rocío.

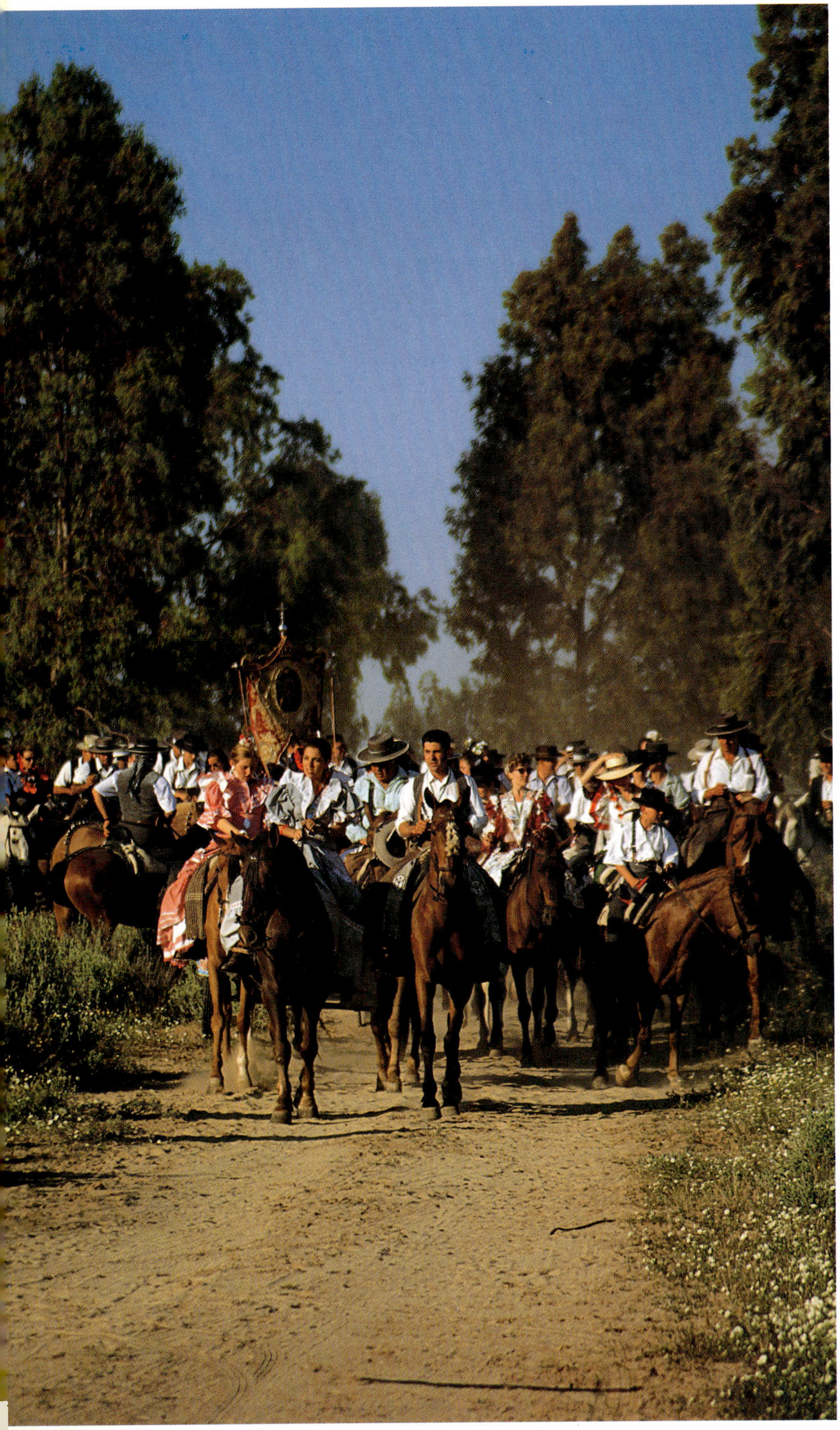

History, Catholicism and paganism: these are the moving forces behind the hundreds of Andalusian festivals, from the commemoration of Judas' punishment to the remembrance of the reconquest of Granada, from the glorification of the Guadalquivir to the *romerías* (pilgrimages). The pilgrimages are probably more pagan than might be expected from a religious festival. Two of them are the most popular in Andalusia: the Romería to the Santuario de la Virgen de la

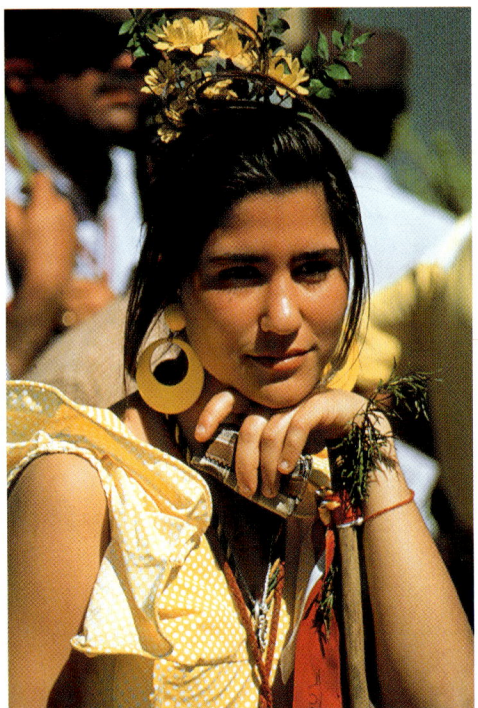

Cabeza in the province of Jaén and the extraordinary Romería al Rocío, in the heart of the Coto Doñana. The latter is undoubtedly the more significant of the two. Legend and history contend for the origins of this unbelievable reunion of devotees in the tiny village of Ayamonte lost in the wilds. It is said that in the 16th century a statue of the Virgin Mary was found in the wood near the Rocina and taken from there to the top of the hill where the sanctuary now stands. History, on the other hand, tells us that Alfonso X had built

130 top and 130-131 As Rocío is situated in the center of Coto Doñana nature park, the roads the pilgrims have to travel cross sandy deserts, water courses and marshes making the trip already filled with enthusiasm even more adventurous.

131 top The church of Rocío seems a neat white brushstroke against the sand and sky. The crowd throngs the entrance in order to see the Vergine return after being abducted on the Sunday night.

131 bottom Rocío pilgrimage has its roots in an event that straddles history and myth. It combines intense religious fervor with the ever-present Andalusian vitality. This is a wonderful chance to wear gypsy dress and adorn a cart with flowers and a horse with all colors of the rainbow - in short, to celebrate.

a statue of the Virgin in this area where he often went hunting. Whatever the origin of the statue, the Virgen del Rocío or Paloma Blanca (white dove), also Andalusia's patron saint, is worshipped and carried in procession at Pentecost. The reason the Virgin is celebrated on the occasion of the descent of the Holy Spirit to the Apostles is one of the contradictory mysteries that make the phenomenon interesting. The most important feature of the celebration, however, is the way in which it is performed. Thousands of pilgrims, many affiliated to more than 80 confraternities, arrive from all over the country and by every mode of transport – by car, on foot, on carts and on horseback – simply dressed or in their best clothes, covering mile after mile of dust and sand to worship the "white dove". The carts and horses, decorated with flowers and garlands and filled with happy pilgrims, rise and fall as they make their way over the dunes of the Coto Doñana while the line of cars moves at a snail's pace through the heat of early June. Many travel for days, camping where they can, dancing and drinking wherever they stop for the night. This continues until the Sunday night when the Virgin is abducted from the sanctuary in an uncontrollable frenzy of worship and religious fervor. The heart of the meaning of so much passion is far from understood. Through a desire to over-analyze, sociology often ends up without explanations and history take its place: al-Andalus is the happy synthesis of great civilizations.

INDEX

Page numbers followed by "c"
  refer to captions.

Page numbers in bold refer to chapters
  dealing with the corresponding
  subject.

136 Two splendid young Andalusian girls are dressed to the nines for the Seville Fair. One of the most Andalusian modes of enjoyment, festivals are a major aspect of this people's culture.

ILLUSTRATION CREDITS

Antonio Attini / Archivio White Star: pages 1, 3-6, 8-9, 10 top, 10-11, 12 left, 13 top, 14, 15, 16-17, 27 bottom, 50 top left, 52-53, 56-57, 58, 59, 60, 60-61, 61, 62 top, 64 top, 65 top and center, 66, 67 top left, 68 top right, 69 top, 70 right, 71, 72, 72-73, 73, 74, 75, 76, 77, 78 top, 79 top, 80, 80-81, 83 top, 84, 85, 86 top right, 86-87, 88, 88-89, 90 top right and left, 90-91, 91 top, 92, 93, 94, 95, 96-97, 97, 98, 99-102, 103, 104, 105, 106, 107, 108, 109, 110, 111, 112, 113, 114, 115, 116, 117, 118 bottom, 118-119, 119, 131, 136.

AKG Photo: page 49 center.

John Bradley / Tony Stone Images / Laura Ronchi: page 81 top.

Michelle Chaplow / Andalucia Slide Library: pages 12-13, 50 center left, 50 bottom right, 50-51, 51 top, 54 bottom, 56 top, 57 top and bottom, 68 top left, 89 top left and right, 91 bottom, 121 top left and right, 122, 123, 127, 128.

Giovanni Dagli Orti: pages 24-25, 30-31, 31 top, 41, 46-47.

Ag. Double's: pages 26-27, 28-29, 30 top, 36 top, 38 center, 40 center, 42 center, 46 bottom.

E.T. Archive: pages 24 top, 33 top, 35 top, 40 top, 44.

Fototeca Storica Nazionale: pages 42 top left, 43 top right, 48 top.

Robert Frerck / Tony Stone Images / Laura Ronchi: page 67 top right.

Angelo Gandolfi: page 53 right.

Gräfenhain Bildagentur Huber / SIME: pages 76-77.

Johanna Huber / SIME: page 63 bottom.

Index Fototeca: pages 22 right, 32-33, 36 bottom, 38 top left, 47 bottom.

Institut Amatller d'Art Hispanic: pages 20 top, 21 bottom right, 22 center, 23 bottom, 32 top left and right, 32 bottom, 35 bottom, 37, 38 bottom, 40 bottom, 42-43, 46 top.

L.A.R.A.: pages 2-7, 22 left, 38-39, 42 bottom, 45.

Mary Evans Picture Library: pages 39 bottom, 49 top and bottom.

Photo Ni matallah / Ag. Luisa Ricciarini: page 26 top.

Ag. Luisa Ricciarini / Milano: pages 20-21, 21 top left, 23 top, 24 bottom, 25 bottom, 28 top, 34.

Archivio Scala: pages 26 bottom, 28 bottom.

Tony Stone Images/ Laura Ronchi: pages 130-131.

Ripani / SIME: page 8 top.

Guido Alberto Rossi / The Image Bank: pages 82-83.

Giovanni Simeone / SIME: pages 11 right, 50 bottom left, 62-63, 64-65, 65 bottom, 82 top right, 126-127.

David Tack / Tony Stone Images / Laura Ronchi: page 129.

Angelo Tondini / Focus Team: pages 54-55, 55 top, 120, 120-121, 126 top.

Map by Betty Vandone